The
Grace-Filled
LIFE

MAXIE D. DUNNAM

The Grace-Filled LIFE

52 Devotions to Warm Your Heart and Guide Your Path

Read Through the Bible in One Year

ABINGDON PRESS
Nashville

THE GRACE-FILLED LIFE
52 DEVOTIONS TO WARM YOUR HEART AND GUIDE YOUR PATH

This book is printed on acid-free paper.

Application for Library of Congress Cataloging-in-Publication Data has been made.

ISBN 978-1-4267-0682-0

All scripture quotations unless noted otherwise are taken from the New Revised Standard Version of the Bible, copyright 1989, Division of Christian Education of the National Council of the Churches of Christ in the United States of America. Used by permission. All rights reserved.

Scripture quotations marked (KJV) are taken from the King James or Authorized Version of the Bible.

Scripture quotations marked (NKJV) are taken from the New King James Version®. Copyright © 1982 by Thomas Nelson, Inc. Used by permission. All rights reserved.

Scripture quotations marked (NIV) are taken from the Holy Bible, NEW INTERNATIONAL VERSION®. Copyright © 1973, 1978, 1984 by International Bible Society. All rights reserved throughout the world. Used by permission of International Bible Society.

Scripture quotations marked (RSV) are taken from the Revised Standard Version of the Bible, copyright 1952 [2nd edition, 1971] by the Division of Christian Education of the National Council of the Churches of Christ in the United States of America. Used by permission. All rights reserved.

Scripture quotations marked (GNT) are from the Good News Translation in Today's English Version—Second Edition © 1992 by the American Bible Society. Used by Permission.

Scripture quotations marked (ESV) are from The Holy Bible, English Standard Version®, copyright © 2001 by Crossway Bibles, a publishing ministry of Good News Publishers. Used by permission. All rights reserved.

Scripture quotations marked (*THE MESSAGE*) are from *THE MESSAGE*. Copyright © by Eugene H. Peterson 1993, 1994, 1995, 1996, 2000, 2001, 2002. Used by permission of NavPress Publishing Group.

10 11 12 13 14 15 16 17 18 19—10 9 8 7 6 5 4 3 2 1

MANUFACTURED IN THE UNITED STATES OF AMERICA

Introduction: God's Breathed Word

John Wesley, the founder of the Methodist Movement, called himself "a man of one book." He wanted Methodists to be Bible people. In fact, early Methodists were derisively referred to as "Bible moths." Here is a passionate expression of his burning conviction:

> To candid, reasonable men, I'm not afraid to lay open what have been the inmost thoughts of my heart. I have thought, I'm a creature of a day, passing through life as an arrow through the air. I am a spirit come from God, and returning to God; just hovering over the great gulf; till a few moments hence, I am not more seen; I drop into an unchangeable eternity. I want to know one thing—the way to heaven; how to land safe on the happy shore. God himself has condescended to teach the way; for this very end he came from heaven. He hath written it down in a book. O give me that book! At any price, give me the Book of God!
> —preface to *John Wesley's Fifty-Three Sermons*, edited by Edward H. Sugden (Nashville: Abingdon Press, 1983)

The Christian movement is always less than it is called to be and has the potential of being what Wesley's kind of conviction demands. For Christians, the Bible is the Word of God, which is "able to instruct you for salvation through faith in Christ Jesus" (2 Tim. 3:15). In fact, it is more than a book; it is, as Paul said to Timothy, "God-breathed, and is useful for teaching, rebuking, correcting and training in righteousness, so that the man of God may be thoroughly equipped for every good work" (2 Tim. 3:16-17 NIV). All that we need for our salvation is in this book. All that we need for growth in discipleship is here. All that we need to be equipped for every good work is here.

It is more than a book: it is revelation and an encounter with the living God. As Christians, we believe the Bible is God's chosen means of self-communication. So in Scripture we encounter the living God.

More than a book, the Bible is an invitation—an invitation to life. The great events of the Old Testament—creation, covenant, and exodus—all reflect the gospel. The movement of God is a movement of love toward us. The big story of the Bible is the story of God staying with us—through his grace wooing us, loving us, seeking to restore us to our created image and bring us back into fellowship with him.

More than a book, the Bible provides the dynamic of faith and hope for a desperate people and a desperate world. G. K. Chesterton was right when he declared, "Christianity, even when watered down, is hot enough to boil all modern society to rags." And the power of it is in God's breathed word.

These devotions seek to capture the dynamic of God's breathed word. There are fifty-two of them, coming from a "reading the Bible through in a year" plan.

This plan is printed as an appendix on pages 173-75. I have selected passages from each week's readings on which to base my devotional reflection. You do not have to read all the suggested passages for each week to get the meaning of the devotions, though you do need to read the designated passages connected with each devotion.

Each devotion has a "life of its own"; therefore, you can use the book as you wish. You may connect it with the plan of reading the Bible through in a year, or you may use it in other ways simply as a part of your devotional life. It is designed to invite and challenge you to make Scripture reading and reflection a part of your daily and weekly discipline for spiritual growth.

I find it meaningful to use different translations in reading and studying Scripture. Also, I recommend a good study Bible—one that has commentary and study helps. There are a number available, but I am especially excited about the *Wesley Study Bible* (Abingdon Press, 2009).

If you give it a chance, by reading it faithfully, you will discover that the Bible is more than a book. It is a revelation and an encounter with the living God. It is an invitation—an invitation to salvation and eternal life. And it is a blueprint for living. Within it is the guide for the way we are to pattern our lives, and at the heart of it is a call to holiness. My prayer is that these devotions will warm your heart and guide your path to a grace-filled life.

Introduction: God's Breathed Word

1

In the Beginning, God

Genesis is a book of "beginnings." This is the meaning of the Greek title *genesis*. This first book of the Bible presents the beginning, the origin of everything *except* God.

Few phrases have stimulated the mind and imagination as this one has: "In the beginning, God." Poets have tried to describe in their words that day. The famous nineteenth-century poet Percy Shelley labeled it the day "when God first dawned on chaos." Artists have tried to paint it. Philosophers have sought to explain it. Scientists have never lost interest in it. Theologians continue to seek and communicate its meaning.

GOD OF BEGINNINGS

In this beginning phrase of the Bible, the first profound truth of Christian understanding is stated: God is eternal.

Perhaps some of your children have asked, "Who made God?" The answer is, "No one. God has always been, God is, and God will always be; he was before the world and before human history, and he will be after the world and human history are dissolved."

Once Martin Luther was asked what God was doing before the world was made. The old reformer replied, "Cutting switches with which to flog those who ask foolish questions!" We may not silence this question in such a harsh way, but for Christians the beginning, the continuing, and the end is God. God is eternal.

Intrigue with these first words of Genesis and the story of creation has not diminished through the years. But neither has its joy. God speaks, and everything changes at once—from nothing to everything, from chaos to order. And at the height of creation: humankind, in God's own image—from the dust of the earth.

When Job was wrestling with the tragic dimensions of his own life, and was debating God, God reminded him of this joyful beginning by asking:

Where were you when I laid the foundation of the earth?
Tell me, if you have understanding.
Who determined its measurements—surely you know! . . .
On what were its bases sunk,
or who laid its cornerstone? (Job 38:4-7)

But joy is soon diminished by the pathos of love and hate, all the human vices and glories in everyday living. Before the end of Genesis 3, the entire gamut of our human experience is recorded, the rich intimacy and harmony of human relationships, even harmony with the earth and its creatures; and paramount, harmony with God. Then comes "the Fall." Adam and Eve, thinking they are wiser than God, do precisely what he commands them not to do. They are left with shame and brokenness, the loss of intimacy with God and others. Life "east of Eden" results.

BUT WE FALL

Karl Barth was one of the most outstanding theologians of the twentieth century. He was a pastor of a village church in Switzerland when World War I came and seemingly all the lights went out. A great darkness descended upon Europe. As pastor, he heard his people crying for some word from the Lord that would make sense out of what had happened. Barth had been raised and trained in the optimistic humanism of the nineteenth century; therefore, he was bereft of anything to preach that would be relevant to the world in which his people lived. In desperation, he turned to the Scripture and discovered what he called "the strange new world within the Bible." From that experience, he wrote *The Word of God and the Word of Man*. He called what he discovered in the Bible "strange" because it described a world of glaring sin and darkness unlike the image of the world held by his confident teachers. He found a diagnosis of the human condition that offered a source for the chaos of his time.

Creation, fall, and redemption are the core themes of Scripture. In the beginning, God. God created, and what God created was and is good. God created humankind, breathed into them his own breath, the breath of life. God gave us freedom, and in our pride we chose to violate God's direction for us; thus, sin came into the world. From then until now—and it will be so until God brings his story to an end—we live with sin at the very heart of our lives. Our only hope is the salvation that is ours through God's gift of himself in Jesus Christ. This is the gospel about which Paul said, "I am not ashamed . . . it is the power of God for salvation to everyone who has faith" (Rom. 1:16).

GOD'S GOODNESS DESPITE OUR DARKNESS

We need to light up another facet of the Creation story that is worthy of reflection. Note the recurring phrase in the Genesis story: "And it was good." Then at the end of the story are the words: "God saw everything that he had made, and indeed, it was very good" (1:31).

We need to hang on to that because the temptation is to see the world and all that is in it as evil. When the darkness of our circumstances makes life seem dark, we grow frightened and sometimes faithless. We find it difficult to believe that God is near and that God has not forgotten us. We long for light in the midst of our darkness. Do you remember John Keats's poem "Ode to a Nightingale"? In the poem, Keats expresses his longing to escape from his pain and join the pleasant-sounding nightingale who flies above the dreary life of human beings. He asks for a cup of poison to drink as he is overwhelmed by emptiness, darkness, meaninglessness, and hopelessness.

That happens to us, doesn't it? The darkness of our particular circumstances makes us believe that all of life is dark, and so we are frightened and sometimes faithless. What we need to know is that God owns the dark as well as the light and is present in the night as well as in the day. God promises to be with us and bring us out of our darkness into the light of his salvation. God's good gift of joy will always be the last word.

QUESTIONS FOR REFLECTION

Where do you need a fresh start? What is the darkest place in your life in which you need God's light to shine?

2

WHAT'S IN A NAME?

GENESIS 4:1-16; JOB 3:1-12

At the very beginning of history, the story of humankind, our story, is acted out not only in Adam and Eve but also in their sons, Cain and Abel. There is a lesson even in their names. Cain means "I have gotten a man." Eve, the proud mother, suggests that this son will bear the dignity of being the firstborn, and that for her he is to be the quintessence of power and strength. "Abel," on the other hand, means something like "nothingness," "frailty," or "meaning-lessness." The younger brother is overshadowed by the elder from the very beginning. He is the representative of those who get the short end of the stick.

BLESSING OR PRIVILEGE

Life is that way, isn't it? There are those who are born with silver spoons in their mouths, and there are those for whom the cry of hunger never ceases.

Cain, as a name and a symbol, speaks volumes to us. The strong ones—the firstborn, the blessed, the ones who have everything—easily find themselves in the center of things.

Here is a challenge for us. We have to be careful that we do not confuse blessing with privilege. Because we are especially blessed—economically, educationally, culturally—does not mean we should have privileges that others don't have. The movie *Driving Miss Daisy* is a marvelous story that makes this lesson clear. Miss Daisy is a Jewish woman—a rich widow. She's stubborn, independent, frugal, and eccentric in a charming way. Her son hires a chauffeur, Hoke, a warm, gentle black man. And that's the story—the story of a rich relationship that grows from Hoke "driving Miss Daisy."

A particularly moving scene is when Hoke drives Miss Daisy to a dinner where Martin Luther King is speaking. The setting is a private Atlanta club, the picture of wealth and Southern elegance. Miss Daisy listens to King in person; Hoke listens on the radio in the car outside. It is obvious that Miss Daisy wishes she had brought Hoke in with her as King speaks those prophetic words, "God's judgment will not alone be upon those who did violence and provoked anger, but also upon those people of good will who knew what was right and good but refused to speak and act for the cause of justice and brotherhood." That got to Miss Daisy.

Another moving scene is the closing one when Miss Daisy has lost her mental faculties. When Hoke comes in for his day's work, he finds her out of touch

The Grace-Filled Life

with reality. She thinks she is a young woman again, teaching school. But Hoke is kind and gentle, listens to her, and calls her to her senses. When she finally is back in touch with reality, she is seated in a chair, Hoke standing beside her. She reaches up with her frail, white, wrinkled hand, and takes his big, boney, black one and says from the depth of her being, "Hoke, you're the best friend I have."

Miss Daisy learned that because we are blessed, it doesn't give us special privileges at the expense of denying them to others. We need to learn that. Because we have everything, we dare not always put ourselves, as Cain did, in the center of the picture.

WHEN THINGS DON'T GO OUR WAY

Now, a second lesson from the Cain and Abel story. When things don't go our way, we are too often quick to blame God. The lesson is in the mysterious story of God accepting Abel's offering but refusing Cain's.

"Abel was a keeper of sheep, and Cain a tiller of the ground." The scripture says, "Cain brought to the LORD an offering of the fruit of the ground, and Abel for his part brought of the firstlings of his flock" (Gen. 4:3-4). Then there is this stark word in verses four and five: "And the LORD had regard for Abel and his offering, but for Cain and his offering he had no regard."

Both men were grateful to God and, at least on the surface, were bringing a fitting sacrificial gift. It's hardly any wonder that "Cain was very angry, and his countenance fell."

Divorce yourself from that quick identification with Cain and think for a moment. Isn't it true that when God takes the liberty to do something that we do not understand and that we think goes against us, we are immediately ready with the question, "How can God do such a thing?"

Think of Job. He believed it was right for the good to prosper and the wicked not to prosper. As long as God conformed to this favorite idea of his, to his conception of a moral world order, he was all right. But when God did something that did not fit into his system of convictions—when Job's children died, his house was burned down, and his flocks were destroyed—he not only withdrew into the sulking corner of his religious house of belief, he questioned God and the meaning of his own life, as would many of us.

Job asked the same question most of us ask at one time or another: Why? At first he tried to keep a stiff upper lip when he said, "The LORD gave, and the LORD has taken away; blessed be the name of the LORD" (1:21). But after Satan was allowed to take Job's health away as well, he begins to cry out in chapter 3 and raise the question over and over: Why? "Why did I not die at birth, / come forth from the womb and expire? Why were there knees to receive me, or breasts for me to suck?" (Job 3:11-12).

It's so with all of us, isn't it? Why should this happen to me? Why did God allow my wife to die so young? Why have my children turned their backs on the church and all I believe? Why is my friend caught in the tenacious clutches of drugs? We identify with what Alex Haley said about the turtle who found himself atop a six-foot fence post in a bean field: "He didn't get where he was all by himself." We know that about our situations. We didn't get here by ourselves, so we blame God.

Cain, unable to understand why his gift is not accepted, stands before the altar of God with a doubting and rebellious heart. God is not acting according to his program. And so Cain reflects our own egotism and lack of trust. Though there is mystery here as to why God accepted Abel's offering but not Cain's, we are led to believe that God was looking on the heart, the attitude of the giver, rather than on the specifics of his offering.

WHAT IS ACCEPTABLE TO GOD?

In the way of money, it's not the amount but the spirit in which you give. And it also has something to do with proportion. That's the reason Jesus made the woman who gave pennies in the temple one of the most famous women in Scripture. She gave everything.

But money is not all we can offer God on the altar. We can offer him our time and energy. We can give God our intentions. We need to be disciplined in our intentions.

We will never be loving extensions of the ministry of Jesus until we become intentional about paying attention to people we meet daily, listening to them, giving them our time. The offering of our life will be acceptable to God only as we are intentional in making that offering daily.

QUESTIONS FOR REFLECTION

Are there circumstances or problems in your life for which you are tempted to blame God? What sin is lurking in your heart?

What privileges are you blessed with? What gifts will you give to God today?

3

GOD KNOWS WHO I AM

PSALM 8; ISAIAH 12

Psalm 8 is one of my favorite psalms. When I'm feeling blue and lonely, when I become preoccupied with failure, and when depression threatens to turn the sky of my life into clouds of grey, I shower my mind with a portion of this psalm.

> When I look at your heavens, the work of your fingers,
> the moon and stars that you have established;
> what are human beings that you are mindful of them,
>   mortals that you care for them?
> Yet you have made them a little lower than God,
>   and crowned them with glory and honor. (Ps. 8:3-5)

It's a thrilling reminder that God knows who I am. And when I think that way, if I am alone, I shout "hallelujah." If I'm where I can't shout, I allow my inner self to sing with joy, otherwise I might explode.

LIVING A HALLELUJAH LIFE

Singing, shouting, celebrating—it's the response of anyone, especially Christians, when contemplating God's story. The psalms are songs—songs that express every mood and attitude of persons. The highs and the lows, the successes and the sorrows, the doubts and the disillusionments are all there. So you have pensive confession, desperate longing for God's presence, honest questioning of God's activity, helpless dependency on God's strength, abandonment of self to God's will and way—and punctuating it all are exclamations of joy.

The coming of Jesus makes the singing more vibrant because we are now even more confident of God's character—his love and grace.

No question about it, the religion of the psalmist is a religion that sings. Psalm 8 is a pristine example. It begins and ends with that exulting greeting, "O LORD, our Sovereign, / how majestic is your name in all the earth!" (vv. 1, 9).

The postmodernists are right when they tell us that modernity—life based solely on science, rationality, and reason—has failed us. Researchers in physics and math are creating and making more space for wonder, imagination, mystery, and majesty. Science itself is discovering that while facts are important, facts alone are not enough either to explain or to experience the mystery and majesty of creation and this magnificent planet that is our dwelling place.

Evolution and intelligent design theories will continue to be debated. They deal with the "how" questions. Faith asks "why" questions dealing with the meaning and purpose of it all, our place as human beings in the "great scheme of it all."

Two of the best-known verses of Scripture are in this psalm. "O LORD, our Lord, / How excellent is Your name in all the earth" (v. 1 NKJV) and "What is man that You are mindful of him?" (v. 4 NKJV). Do you see it? It is only in the context of praising God, certainly only after praising him, that we can rightfully consider who we are. The psalmist places humanity within the vastness of God's creation. At first glance, that vastness highlights the smallness of humans. The motive of the psalmist is brilliant. He wants us to see God's immense care and concern for us, so he marvels, "What are human beings that you are mindful of them, / mortals that you care for them?"

Our marveling at the heavens, the work of God's fingers, might well be beyond that of the psalmist. We have far more data than was available to David's naked eye. We know that in one second a beam of light travels 186,000 miles, which is seven times greater than the distance around the earth. It takes eight minutes for that beam to go from the sun to the earth. That beam from sun to earth travels almost six trillion miles in a year. Scientists call this a light-year. It boggles the mind. Eight billion light-years from the earth is halfway to the edge of the known universe. There are a hundred billion galaxies, each with a hundred billion stars, on average, within the universe. There are perhaps as many planets as stars within all the galaxies—ten billion trillion!

With our heads spinning, we ask with the psalmist, "What is man . . . ?" The psalmist doesn't give us all the answers, but he gives us enough to go on. He says we are made a little less than God, and that we are crowned with glory and honor. That means you and me. That puts us in our place—a wonderful place in relation to God. A part of what that means is in the question of the psalmist: "What is man that You are mindful of him?" The adjective *mindful* derives from the verb *remember* (*zakar*). Take heart: we are remembered by God. God knows who we are.

LIFT UP YOUR HEART

"What is man that you are mindful of him, / And the son of man that You visit him?" (NKJV). Visit here means "to attend to, to observe," so the NRSV has it "mortals that you care for them." Lift up your heart. Rise from any cowering back in self-disdain or self-depreciation. God has his eye on you. Even when we forget, he remembers. Even when we get lost and wander away, he keeps us in mind. He knows who we are.

The Grace-Filled Life

The prophet Isaiah kept reminding Israel that God would not forget the nation he had chosen to be an instrument of his redemption. As he preached to Israel, he sang a song of thanksgiving and praise.

Surely God is my salvation;
 I will trust, and will not be afraid,
for the LORD God is my strength and my might;
 he has become my salvation. (12:2)

Isaiah was confident that there is no way for us to get beyond the scope of God's love.

"The Lord of hosts is mustering an army for battle" (Isa. 13:4b). God always acts to redeem and rescue us. We can't outrun, out-give, outlast, or outgrow God's love. Out of the depth of that love, God delivered the people of God out of Egypt, moved an army to deliver the people of God from exile, and later would send the Son to rescue the world. The whole of Scripture captures God's great love affair with humanity. We may try to run and hide, but the arm of God's love for us is always long enough to reach and rescue us. (*Wesley Study Bible*, Life Application Topic: "Love of God," p. 830)

The final answer to the question "What is man . . . ?" is answered in Jesus. In all sorts of ways he answers the question, but in one particular way he gives us the answer of who we are by telling us who God is. Jesus called God, "Abba, Father" (Mark 14:36). He taught us to pray, "Our Father . . ." (Matt. 6:9). Don't forget: we are God's children. God knows who we are.

Loving God can even help us love one another more or even at all. Loving God and accepting God's grace with all of our heart, soul, mind, and strength will restore us to a right relationship with God. And it will also help us love ourselves and other people.

QUESTIONS FOR REFLECTION

Do you really believe God is Abba, Father, and loves you? Who do you need to love more? Who do you need to remember in prayer? How will you praise God with your life today?

4

LIFE ISN'T FAIR, BUT LIFE ISN'T GOD

JOB 7:1-19; ROMANS 8:31-39

WHY IS THERE PAIN AND SUFFERING?

An interesting twist of response to tragedy came years ago when United Airlines Flight 232 crashed in Sioux City, Iowa. Survivors attributed their survival to God. An organization of atheists, known as the Freedom from Religion Foundation, issued a call for secular newspapers to quit using "Bible Belt journalism." Ann Gaylor, leader of the group, said, "Every time a tragedy is reported our members must brace themselves for the inevitable. If there are survivors, reporters will make sure God will get the credit, but never the blame. Why don't they ask these religionists who claim God helped them why he let tragedies happen in the first place?" Referring to the United crash she asked, "Why didn't their omnipotent God just fix the hydraulic system of United Flight 232 and save everybody?" ("News Report's Mention of God Angers Atheists," *Atlanta Constitution*, August 12, 1989).

This is the question of the book of Job. Why? Why do bad things happen to good people? More expansive than that, why is there pain and suffering in the world? Wrestling with the devastation of his life—his oxen, camels, and donkeys stolen and his servants killed; sheep and other servants burned up by fire from heaven; his sons and daughters destroyed by a storm—Job struggled with the why of it all. Early on in his tormented struggle he moaned,

> The arrows of the Almighty are in me;
> > my spirit drinks their poison;
> > the terrors of God are arrayed against me. . . .
> O that I might have my request . . .
> that it would please God to crush me . . .
> This would be my consolation;
> > I would even exult in unrelenting pain;
> > for I have not denied the words of the Holy One. (6:4, 8-10)

In a kind of sneer, he turns a portion of Psalm 8 into a parody, accusing God of paying too much attention to him.

> What are human beings, that you make so much of them,
> > that you set your mind on them,

visit them every morning,
> test them every moment? (Job 7:17-18)

Who would dare speak to God in this fashion? Only a person of faith. Job is a model for us. He is overwhelmed by his suffering. He doesn't understand it. He searches his soul to discover any sin of which he is unaware, then pleads with God that if there is any sin why doesn't God pardon, rather than pile suffering upon suffering.

> If I sin, what do I do to you, you watcher of humanity?
> Why have you made me your target? (7:20)

Job is asking the same question most of us ask at one time or another: Why? The question will continue to haunt us, and we may never find a satisfactory answer to the expansive issue of evil and suffering in the world. We all know this: life isn't fair, but we need to keep reminding ourselves that life isn't God.

GOD *IS* FOR US

Honesty is essential in our relationship to life and to God. We must own who we are, the circumstances of our life, and keep a clear perspective about the character of God. We have what Job did not have—a clear revelation of God in Jesus Christ, which gives us the confidence of Paul that "in everything God works for good with those who love him" (Rom. 8:28 RSV).

Paul asks a number of questions in this Romans passage. Two of them, in particular, give us perspective. One, "If God is for us, who is against us?" (v. 31b). Paul doesn't want his readers to miss the powerful affirmation he is giving through the question, so he uses an allusion from sacred history that would immediately grab the attention of his Jewish audience. "He who did not withhold his own Son, but gave him up for all of us, will he not with him also give us everything else?" (v. 32).

Think of the greatest example you know of a person's loyalty to God. Think of Abraham, Paul is saying. God's love and loyalty to us is like that. Just as Abraham was so faithful and trustful to God—willing to sacrifice his only son for God—God is so loving and faithful that he sacrificed his only Son. If a God like that is for us, who can be against us?

The second question, "Who will separate us from the love of Christ?" (v. 35). For the question to burrow its way into our minds, Paul names those things that threaten us: tribulation, distress, persecution, famine, nakedness—all the perils of human life; included in that for us would be heart attack, stroke, cancer, surgery, war, tornadoes, earthquakes. Can these separate us from the love of Christ? Paul shouts his answer: "No, in all these things we are more than conquerors through him who loved us" (v. 37).

Life isn't fair, but life isn't all there is. In all the "whys" of life, we can be more than conquerors. We appropriate that truth by using our circumstances, whether pain and suffering or affirmation and joy, to more consciously claim the love of Christ.

QUESTIONS FOR REFLECTION

Where have you been treated unfairly? God is for you and for me. How can this promise help you meet life's difficulties? Where do you need God's friendship today?

5

THERE IS A PRICE

JOSHUA 23:14-16; JOSHUA 24:19-27; MATTHEW 13:44-47

There is an old adage that has God saying, "Take what you wish . . . and pay for it!" It's true. There is a price for everything.

To be sure, the beauty of God's creation is a gift. Yet there is a "price" to pay if we are going to really enjoy it. We are often dull to beauty, with no eyes to see, because we don't take time to sit quietly and take in the beauty that God is offering us through his creation. The fact is those things we think are free, indeed, those things given as gift, require something from us to fully appreciate them. There is a price—a price for everything.

In chapter 13 of his Gospel, in just four verses, Matthew records three parables of Jesus. In these three brief parables, there are two big lessons. One, no entrance price to the Kingdom is too great, and two, there will be a time of judgment.

In the first parable, a man, by chance, found a treasure hidden in a field and sold everything in order to raise the money to purchase the field. In the second parable, a merchant seeking fine pearls found one pearl of such value that he sold all he had and bought it.

Jesus is talking about the Kingdom, our living in the realm of the Lordship of Christ. There is a price for that. Whatever it takes to enter, whatever cost may be exacted from us, the Kingdom of God is worth it.

WHERE IS YOUR TREASURE?

The overarching lesson of the parable of the treasure in the field and the pearl of great price is that no entrance price to the kingdom is too great. The merchant seeking fine pearls demonstrates this lesson differently than the farmer. Two truths loom large in the story: one, we are likely to find what we search for persistently; and two, we are likely to receive what we want passionately.

Now back to the central point of these parables. Why did Jesus tell two parables at the same time with the same message? He didn't want anyone to miss the point. Anyone, everyone, the rich and the poor receive the Kingdom the same way—*by making it the priority of their lives.*

Joshua had a vision of this as it related to Israel and Israel's faithfulness. As he came to the end of his life, he reminded the people that what appears to be an unconditional promise of faithfulness on God's part is, in fact, conditional.

This is the message of the whole of Scripture. God's promises to act in our individual lives and in history are often connected with conditions we are to meet. So Joshua reiterated the case: Israel's devotion or lack of devotion will determine whether or not the Lord's promise will be realized. "You know in your hearts and souls . . . that not one thing has failed of all the good things that the LORD your God promised concerning you" (Josh. 23:14).

But it might not always be that way. If Israel turned away from God to idolatry, "just as all the good things that the LORD your God promised . . . so the LORD will bring upon you all the bad things" (23:15). And just before his death, Joshua reaffirmed Israel's covenant with God and put a huge stone of reminder in the sanctuary and announced to all the people,

> "See, this stone shall be a witness against us; for it has heard all the words of the LORD that he spoke to us; therefore it shall be a witness against you, if you deal falsely with your God." (24:27)

The stone would be a visible reminder and witness against the Israelites if they strayed from the Lord.

Jesus' third parable about the Kingdom, then, should not be a surprise. The parable of the fishing net tells us there will be a time of separation, a time of judgment. Jesus' language is as "hard" as Joshua's. The angels will "separate the evil from the righteous and throw them into the furnace of fire, where there will be weeping and gnashing of teeth" (Matt. 13:49-50). It's a sobering picture, and it leaves us with a searching question: Is the way we live affected at all by the fact that one day we are going to stand before the judgment bar of God and give an account of our deeds?

QUESTIONS FOR REFLECTION

What good things have come your way that you didn't expect or plan? God is your friend, but how good a friend are you to God? What steps do you need to take to live a life more pleasing to God?

6

CURIOSITY OR CONSECRATION?

GENESIS 22:9-19; MATTHEW 16:24-28; ROMANS 12:1-8

In the second act of the play *Gideon*, by Paddy Chayefsky, an angel of the Lord recognizes that Gideon has rejected him. Gideon vacillates between love and disenchantment, between a desire to serve and a longing to be served. Finally, he turns away from the Lord's representative, and the angel speaking for the Lord says, "I meant for you to love me, but you were only curious."

FROM THE TOP OF YOUR HEAD TO THE BOTTOM OF YOUR HEART

Could that be a personal indictment against us? We have been curious but hardly consecrated. We have been flabby in our commitment. The Christian faith and way has been a matter that caught us at the top of our heads but not at the bottom of our hearts. We have time for everything for which those who are not dedicated to the cause of Jesus have time. We surround ourselves with the same luxuries with which those who make no Christian claims surround themselves. What can be said of our Christian faith and commitment when we seek to serve the Kingdom of God with spare money in spare time?

Paul presents a tough challenge. In the first eleven chapters of his Epistle to the Romans he spells out in a clear and convincing way his understanding of the heart of the Christian faith, justification by grace through faith. Now, as he begins the twelfth chapter, he begins to offer practical instruction for how we are to live the new life we have been given by Christ.

> I appeal to you therefore, brothers and sisters, by the mercies of God, to present your bodies as a living sacrifice, holy and acceptable to God, which is your spiritual worship. Do not be conformed to this world, but be transformed by the renewing of your minds, so that you may discern what is the will of God—what is good and acceptable and perfect. (Rom. 12:1-2)

One wonders if Paul is remembering the most vivid demonstration of faithfulness and trust in God we have in all history: the story of Abraham's sacrifice of his son Isaac. It is one of the most powerful, profound, and disturbing stories in the Bible, and in all of literature for that matter. The story of Abraham is the story of a promise. God promises Abraham and Sarah that they would have a child and that their descendants from this child would be as numerous as the stars. Isaac is the promised child.

The story is filled with drama. Abraham is seventy-five years old and Sarah is sixty-five years old when the angel first visits them and tells them they are going to have a baby (Gen. 12:4-8). They trust and follow God's lead, though it is twenty-five years later when the angel returns to tell them, "Get ready; the baby is coming." Abraham is now almost one hundred years old. Sarah is ninety. Abraham and Sarah could not possibly, through biological processes, produce this child.

It would be wonderful, as stories go, for the story to end there—an old couple having a baby! The promise is fulfilled. But it doesn't end there. Now God's word is not a promise but a command that must have taken Abraham's breath away: "Take your son, your only son Isaac, whom you love, and go to the land of Moriah, and offer him there as a burnt offering on one of the mountains that I shall show you" (22:2).

Perhaps more surprising than that horrific command is Abraham's response. He does what the Lord tells him to do. In an almost matter-of-fact way, Abraham follows through to the point of being poised with the knife over the altar where he has bound his child of promise, ready to take the life of his beloved son, his only son. But the Lord intervenes. Abraham has proven his faith and trust, and God provides a substitute offering.

That's our ultimate test. Are we able to let go of everything in the trust that the Lord will deliver on his promise? Do we trust God, who gives the gift in the first place? Was Paul thinking of this when he appealed to the Romans "by the mercies of God" that Christians present themselves as living sacrifices? The image is prominent in the biblical message because it leads us to the Cross, the heart of God's redemptive plan. God provides a substitute for Isaac, but there is no substitute for God's Isaac, his "only begotten Son," Jesus. Jesus knows the Cross is inevitable, and he describes the meaning of discipleship by reference to the cross. "If any want to become my followers, let them deny themselves and take up their cross and follow me" (Matt. 16:24).

With these reflections, the words of the playwright probe to the depth of our being: "I meant for you to love me, but you were only curious."

YOUR SECURITY SYSTEM REVEALED

Some areas of telling concern will not let us escape honest examination. Begin at a very simple level—the daily routine interests of our lives. The things in which persons are daily interested tell the story of their commitment.

The daily routine interests of our life are pretty revealing about our Christian faith and commitment. The priority of those interests is revealed in the way we spend our money. What are the first checks we write each month? Jesus said, "Where your treasure is, there your heart will be also" (Luke 12:34). Think about this: each year we Americans spend $7 billion on tobacco, $9 billion on alcoholic drinks, and $11 billion on vacations, while we spend only $4.5 billion on religion and welfare combined. In a recent year in the United States, we spent $55 million on migrant birds, while we spent $40 million on ministry to migrant farmers. We spent $3 billion on house plants during a year when we spent only $1.7 billion on poverty issues. It's a revealing exercise—just to look at the checks we write.

NOT MY WILL, BUT YOURS, LORD

Probe a bit deeper now. What of our efforts at spiritual maturity? Paul talked about this in different ways. "Present your bodies as a living sacrifice. . . . Do not be conformed to this world, but be transformed by the renewing of your minds." That was his word to the Romans (12:1-2). He urged the Galatians to "grow up in Christ." It was the same longing that he had for the Christians in Ephesus—that they arrive at real "maturity, to the measure of the full stature of Christ" (4:13). Is that a conscious part of our life, a deep desire and a commensurate, deliberate discipline to become a whole person spiritually?

Do you know the story of Frank Laubach? He was known as the apostle to the illiterates and was responsible, through his "each one, teach one" program, for the literacy of millions of people. Developing the inner resources of his life, connected with his burning concern to minister to the world's disinherited, made him sensitive to his needs for an intimate relationship with God. Here is a letter that he wrote very early in his quest for wholeness:

> I climbed Signal Hill today in back of my house—talking and listening to God— all the way up, all the way back, all the lovely half hour spent on the top. A few months ago I was trying to write a chapter on the discovering of God. Now that I have discovered him, I find that it is a continuous discovery, and every day is rich with new aspects of him and his working. If I throw these mind-windows apart and say, God, what shall we think of now? He always answered in a beautiful tender way, and I know that God is love hungry because he is constantly pointing me to some dull dead soul which he has never reached, and wistfully urges me to help him reach that stolid, tight shut mind. (*Letters by a Modern Mystic* [Westwood, N.J.: Fleming H. Revell, 1958], pp. 27-28)

Wholeness comes only through an intentional, intimate, ongoing communion with the living Christ. The one thing that can save us from insignificance is giving ourselves to a cause that is greater than ourselves. Did you ever ask yourself the question, "What does this world, what does the Lord, want of me?" Have you any good reason for going on breathing the air of this world and eating its food and taking up its space?

What area of your life might suggest that your Christian faith and commitment is more curiosity than consecration? What changes are you willing to make? In what areas of your daily life do you need to trust God more?

7

WHAT TO DO WHEN YOU HAVE BEEN FORGIVEN

GENESIS 27:30-40; MATTHEW 18:21-35

In the musical *My Fair Lady*, Professor Henry Higgins, whose heart is being torn apart by Eliza Doolittle, tries to convince himself that he is a forgiving man, in spite of the fact that he finds it almost impossible to forgive Eliza. Like most of us, he can't stick to that understanding of himself as "a most forgiving man," or it doesn't come through with conviction. His temper gets the best of him and he adds an addendum:

> But I will never take her back, if she were crawling on her knees! . . .
> I will slam the door and let the hell cat freeze.

MOST FORGIVING OR MOST FORGIVEN

We know the tension, don't we? The tension between applauding forgiveness in general but refusing to offer forgiveness in specific. Jesus presents our experience in a parable, a drama really, in which we are participants. He told the story in response to Peter's questions, "How often should I forgive? As many as seven times?" Jesus said to him, "Not seven times, but, I tell you, seventy-seven times" (Matt. 18:21-22).

But that wasn't enough for Jesus; he had to make it personal and plain. So he adds a parable. The drama unfolds rapidly, keeping us on the edge of our seats. Our feelings are stirred and change erratically as the drama unfolds. We feel sympathy for the man who owed such a burdensome debt. The king angers us at once because he is going to exact every ounce of life from the debtor. Then abruptly the king becomes a hero, not a villain. We are flabbergasted by his compassion and the extent of his mercy as he forgives the debtor. The forgiven debtor encounters a man who owes him just a pittance and has him thrown into jail, and anger boils over again. Our boiling anger subsides and we breathe a sigh of satisfaction when the king brings the unforgiving debtor back to judgment and delivers him to be tormented until his huge debt is paid.

There is a call here; a call to get on the stage and into the drama. This is the very stuff of life because forgiveness—forgiving and being forgiven—is at the very center of life.

The story of Jacob and Esau (Gen. 27–33) is one of the most poignant biblical witnesses to this. Esau, the elder brother, had all rights to the blessing of their father, Isaac. But Jacob stole that blessing. Jacob had to flee for his life from the natural wrath of Esau. For years Jacob was an alien, removed from his family and his homeland. Finally, he got the courage to run the risk and, with his entire household, returned to the Promised Land. It is one of most inspiring stories in the Old Testament. Forgiveness pierces through the pain and darkness of estrangement. When Esau saw Jacob coming, he "ran to meet him, and embraced him, and fell on his neck and kissed him, and they wept" (Gen. 33:4). A forgiving brother restores life to Jacob and the family.

The theme runs throughout Scripture. The core lesson of the parable is a truth we are lax in reckoning with: God's forgiveness of us is determined by our forgiveness of others. Jesus even included that lesson in the prayer he taught us: "Forgive us . . . as we forgive others."

A TOUCHY TRUTH

This is a touchy truth, not easy to keep clear. Look closely at the parable. No sooner had the servant been forgiven his unpayable debt than he found someone indebted to him. He had been forgiven 10,000 denarii; this man owed him only 100 denarii, yet he had him thrown into jail. No wonder the king was angry and reacted so quickly, having the unforgiving man incarcerated as well. Jesus closed the parable with the words, "So my heavenly Father will also do to every one of you, if you do not forgive your brother or sister from your heart" (Matt. 18:35).

Register this truth quickly. The Bible does not teach of a God who refuses or revokes pardon. God's love is neither conditional nor capricious. So how do we harmonize the truth of this parable with this truth about God's character? Only as we forgive others can God's forgiveness become real. God forgives, but our capacity to receive and retain that forgiveness as a redemptive power in our lives is dependent on our forgiving others. We can't be open to God's love if we continue to bitterly nurse our resentments against someone.

I recall a movie entitled *Stars in My Crown*. The story was especially powerful for one who grew up in the South and knew the integrity of the story, even if it wasn't truly biographical. An elderly black man owned a small, rather unproductive farm outside a Southern town. When some precious metals were discovered in the area, the land suddenly became valuable. Though many sought to buy it, the old man refused to sell. It was his land, his home, and he wanted to stay where he had spent his life. People did everything they could to force him out, but he refused. They burned his barn, shot through his house at night, and, in a final threat, told him he would be hanged by sundown the next day if he did not agree to sell.

The Grace-Filled Life

The local Methodist minister heard about the trouble and went to visit, and an amazing thing happened. As promised, at sundown the next day, they came. Though they were robed in their white sheets and hoods, the old man knew who they were. The farmer came out on the porch, wearing his best clothes. He told them he was ready to die, that he had asked the minister to draw up his last will and testament. He asked the minister to read it to them. He willed the farm to the banker who had been most clamoring in his effort to get it. He gave his rifle to one, who as a little boy had first learned to hunt with that gun, who was taught by the old black man. He gave his fishing pole to another; on and on, giving everything he had to those who were threatening to kill him.

The impact was incredible. He killed them with love and forgiveness. They couldn't take it. One by one, in shame, the lynching mob disappeared. The minister's grandson had watched everything from a distance, and as everyone was leaving, he ran to his grandfather and asked, "What kind of will was that, Granddaddy?" The minister replied, "That, my son, was the will of God."

Doesn't that make you think about Jesus at the Cross? And thinking about the Cross makes us think of God's loving sacrifice. What does all that say to us, about what we are to do when we have been forgiven?

QUESTIONS FOR REFLECTION

Who do you need to forgive? Whose forgiveness do you need?

8

IF ONLY . . . NEXT TIME

ISAIAH 43:1-3, 14-21; ROMANS 15:22-33

If only! We hear it all the time. If only I hadn't had that accident. If only I'd lived in some other place. If only he had not died so young. If only I had more money. If only I were younger. If only I were older. If only I had a different job. If only people really knew me. It goes on and on . . . if only!

A WORLD OF DIFFERENCE

There is a world of difference between if only and next time. If only looks backward; next time looks forward. If only is a phrase of defeat; next time is a phrase of hope. The prophet Isaiah kept reminding Israel that our God is a "next time" God. Isaiah is referred to as "the golden prophet." He rises to great heights in expressing truth in illuminating imagery. That truth was always "Truth," no diminishing of the judgment of God upon Israel because of her lackluster faithlessness, but also no hesitancy about promise and hope.

At the close of Isaiah, in chapters 40–44, he has offers of comfort.

Comfort, O comfort my people, says your God.
Speak tenderly to Jerusalem, . . .
that she has served her term,
    that her penalty is paid. (40:1-2)

And the *assurance* of God's help

Do not fear, for I am with you, . . .
I will strengthen you, I will help you. (41:10)

And *affirmation* as God's servant and witness

I have given you as a covenant to the people,
    a light to the nations,
    to open the eyes that are blind,
to bring out the prisoners from the dungeon,
    from the prison those who sit in darkness. (42:6-7)

And the *promise of unlimited blessing and protection*

Do not fear, for I have redeemed you;
   I have called you by name, you are mine. . . .
when you walk through fire you shall not be burned,
   and the flame shall not consume you. (43:1-2)

After all that, he makes it clear that Israel is called to faithfulness and God is a jealous, demanding God. He gives a scathing denunciation against idolatry.

All who make idols are nothing, and the things they delight in do not profit;
   . . . they will be put to shame. (44:9)

Isaiah keeps the picture clear. God is jealous and demanding. He calls for faithfulness. But he is a "next time" God.

Do not remember the former things,
   or consider the things of old.
I am about to do a new thing;
   now it springs forth, do you not perceive it? (43:18).

Let Isaiah speak to us personally about if only and next time.

FREEDOM FROM REGRET AND SELF-PITY

If only is a life dominated by regret, and regret is a paralyzing emotion. Many of us are its victims. Our lives are dominated by this energy-draining emotion: "If only I hadn't done this" or "If only I had done that" . . . These are useless words. They keep us preoccupied with the past and drain us of the energy needed for present living. If only regrets also blind us to the offer of life and relationship, the opportunities for service and joy that are coming all the time. That's the reason God says to us, "Do not remember the former things. . . . / I am about to do a new thing" (43:18-19).

If only is not only a life dominated by regret; it is always an expression of self-pity, and there is nothing creative or positive about self-pity. Rather, self-pity is debilitating. When we bury ourselves in self-pity, we cut off the creativity and the power that could open doors to new life.

QUESTIONS FOR REFLECTION

What regrets hold you back? What can you do today to trust your "next time" God?

9

THE CROSS: THE POWER AND WISDOM OF GOD

JOHN 18:1-11; 1 CORINTHIANS 1:1-25; 1 CORINTHIANS 2:1-5

John Milton was one of the great English poets. In 1629, he wrote his lovely poem *On the Morning of Christ's Nativity*. A year later, he attempted to write a companion poem entitled *The Passion*. After some eight toilsome verses, he gave up. Sometime later, he wrote these words about the unfinished poem, "The subject that author finding to be above the years he had when he wrote it, and nothing satisfied with what was begun, left it unfinished." Though we are powerless to adequately put into words the full meaning of the Cross, we cannot leave the matter "unfinished" as Milton did. There is something haunting about it that will not let us put it aside.

BEYOND OUR KNOWING

For the message about the cross is foolishness to those who are perishing, but to us who are being saved it is the power of God. (1 Cor. 1:18)

If ever there was a person of one subject, it was Paul. His mind and heart are set like flint: "I decided [Some translations have 'determined.'] to know nothing among you except Jesus Christ, and him crucified" (1 Cor. 2:2). He was confident that the "wisdom" of God was most clearly expressed in the Cross. The depth of this wisdom is beyond what we can fathom; we depend on the Spirit for revelation and the demonstration of the power of the Cross.

A popular monk in the Middle Ages announced that in the cathedral that evening he would preach a sermon on the love of God. The people gathered and stood in silence waiting for the service while the sunlight streamed through the beautiful windows. When the last glint of color had faded from the windows, the old monk took a candle from the altar. Walking to the life-size figure of Christ on the cross, he held the light beneath the wounds of the feet, then His hands, then His side. Still without a word, he let the light shine on the thorn-crowned brow.

That was his sermon. The people stood in silence and wept. They knew they were at the center of mystery beyond their knowing, that they were looking at the love of God, the image of the invisible God giving himself for us—a love so deep, so inclusive, so expansive, so powerful, so complete that the mind could not comprehend nor measure it, nor words express it.

Paul knew that too. He comes back to it again and again: the purpose and power of the Cross. We could explore it from many directions, but let's focus on Christ and the Cross as the power and wisdom of God.

Look for a moment at Jesus just prior to the Cross. He is in the Garden of Gethsemane. He knows that the Cross is imminent, and he is wrestling with it, praying that "the cup" might pass from him. His enemies come with their torches looking for him. They didn't need torches. He was not hiding, but was there in the moonlit openness for all to see.

What *courage*! And what authority! They came in numbers and power. He asked them, "Whom are you looking for?" They responded, "Jesus of Nazareth." With boldness, Jesus said, "I am he." What happened then? Scripture says, "They stepped back and fell to the ground" (John 18:4-6). There was authority in his very being.

The scene shows us that Jesus chose to die. He could have escaped death. He chose to die. He even helped his enemies arrest him. He was utterly obedient. "Am I not to drink the cup that the Father has given me?" (18:11). This was God's will, and that was enough for Jesus.

Earlier in the evening, before his arrest in the garden, Jesus was in the Upper Room with his disciples celebrating Passover together. He confronted Judas with the fact that he was going to betray him. He even gave Judas the command, "Do quickly what you are going to do," (13:27) and the Scripture says that after Judas had received the bread, he went out into the night.

Jesus knew where he was going, what he was going to do, and what it was going to result in—his own crucifixion—the Cross. When this happened with Judas, Jesus said, "Now the Son of Man has been glorified, and God has been glorified in him" (13:31).

GOD'S WISDOM AND POWER

So John presents the Cross as the highest point of Jesus' Glory. With this in mind, let's look at the Cross as the wisdom and power of God.

The Cross is the revelation of God's heart. Here we see that there is more love in God than we can even imagine. That means there is more love in him than there is sin in us. We need to know this because it is quite possible for us to become so aware of our wretched tendency that we grow oblivious to God's redemptive capacity. Jesus did not die on Calvary simply to fulfill prophecy from the Old Testament. Neither did he suffer and die as a human sacrifice to appease an angry deity. The Bible clearly and frequently says that ours is a God of love and mercy. Jesus died on the cross to show the extent to which God will go to reveal to us just how much we are loved. The cross is one of the most dramatic reminders of God's unmerited and unending grace. At the cross, we are assured there is more love in God than sin in us.

Paul says our first need is for forgiveness and power over sin. In Colossians 1:22, he paints a beautiful picture of what the Cross does for us. "He has now reconciled [you] in his body of flesh by his death, in order to present you holy and blameless and irreproachable before him" (RSV).

Put the truth of the Cross as the wisdom and power of God another way. *The Cross is the throne of God's saving power.*

Halford E. Luccock used to laugh at the hymnal that has as number 364 *Jesus Demands My All*; then, at the bottom of the page, it reads, "For an easier version, see Number 365." There is not only no easier version for eternal salvation; there is no *other* version than the Cross of Jesus Christ. The Cross is the throne of God's saving power.

A preacher wrote me a letter expressing his opposition to the position I had taken in my lecture on evangelism. The point that he argued against was my contention that what we think of Jesus Christ will determine what we do about evangelism. I was pleading for a recovery of belief and commitment to the uniqueness of Christ as God's way of salvation for all humankind. I was also calling into question the belief in universal salvation.

The fellow shared a story from a lecture he had heard over twenty years ago. The only thing he remembered about it was the exchange between the theological lecturer and an overly enthusiastic super-evangelical student. The student asked the impertinent question, "When were you saved?" The professor thought for a moment. "When was I saved?" he asked rhetorically, then paused. "I was saved two thousand years ago."

The writer used this to argue against the point of my questioning universal salvation, the belief that eventually everyone is going to be saved. He offered the story to refute my position, but I take it as support. Our salvation occurred two thousand years ago—on the Cross of Jesus. The Cross is the throne of Christ's saving power.

Do you remember the words of the liturgy of Holy Communion? "Jesus Christ who made there, by the one offering of Himself, a full, sufficient sacrifice for the sins of the whole world." So it is; so it shall always be. The Cross is the throne of Christ's saving grace. And, as the revelation of God in Jesus dying on the cross, it tells us that there is more love in God than sin in us.

QUESTIONS FOR REFLECTION

What does it mean to be a Christian with power and authority? There is more love in God than there is sin in us: how might the truth of this statement affect your life today? How does what we think of Christ influence how we witness and how the church practices evangelism?

The Grace-Filled Life

10

THE GREAT COMMISSION

MATTHEW 28:16-20

The last words of Jesus to his disciples represent the marching orders that are to be followed until he returns. We call it "the great commission." Wise observers of the mainline denominations have said "the great commission" has become our "great omission." There is not a single major mainline church that is growing significantly in membership in the United States. At least four of the major mainline denominations—Presbyterians, Episcopalians, Lutherans, and Methodists—have internal battles that threaten schism.

JESUS' MINISTRY—AND OURS

At the beginning of his ministry, Jesus announced his mission:

The Spirit of the Lord is upon me, because he hath anointed me to preach the gospel to the poor; he hath sent me to heal the brokenhearted, to preach deliverance to the captives, and recovering of sight to the blind, to set at liberty them that are bruised, to preach the acceptable year of the Lord. (Luke 4:18-19 KJV)

At the close of his ministry, Jesus commissions us for Kingdom work:

Go therefore and make disciples of all nations, baptizing them in the name of the Father and of the Son and of the Holy Spirit, teaching them to observe all things that I have commanded you; and lo, I am with you always, even to the end of the age. (Matt. 28:19-20 NKJV)

Register what should be obvious: only disciples can make disciples. Our mission statement in The United Methodist Church is "To make disciples of Jesus Christ for the transformation of the world." Discipleship means following Jesus to the end that we are transformed into his likeness. Here is our problem. Most members of our churches do not have any compelling sense that their primary vocation as Christians is to practice those disciplines that will form them into the likeness of Christ—that the dynamic of being a Christian is the understanding of and conformity to the clear teachings of Jesus.

DISCIPLE-MAKING

Making disciples, then, is more than making "converts." How have we missed the point that the command of Jesus is to "make disciples"? Salvation is for more than forgiveness; it is also a matter of thorough moral and spiritual transformation.

Over 150 million people in America claim to be "born again" Christians. We have to question what that means. If all "born again Christians" were disciples, would there not be greater signs of the transforming power of Christ at work in the world?

Another problem is that, too often, in mainline churches, we have substituted an ideological social agenda for the Christian gospel. When our mission agenda is only a social action program that is devoid of any acknowledgment of sin and satanic power, then there is no need for repentance and forgiveness.

Religious pluralism and inclusivism have played havoc with our mission enterprise. Pluralism denies Jesus as God's unique gift of salvation, and inclusivism offers universal salvation. When these prevail, there is no passion for the Great Commission. We cannot denigrate the uniqueness of Christ as God's way of salvation, diminish the authority of Scripture, or idealize pluralism and inclusiveness as redemptive within themselves and have anything that will demand commitment, sacrifice, and a response to the call to go to the ends of the earth to share it.

Most observers of the Christian scene in the United States would contend that we are in a setting not much different from the time when Jesus gave the Great Commission. That means we must become "apostolic" in our passion and style of sharing the gospel.

Seventy million individuals in the United States are under the age of eighteen. Nearly one million foreign-born people immigrate to this country every year. Thirty-two million people in America speak some language other than English as their primary language. We have more unsaved and unchurched people in our nation than ever before in our history—172 million. Ninety percent of the population of the United States lives in urban settings. The Great Commission and an apostolic style demand that we "go to" all of these persons, not wait for them to come to us.

PASSION FOR SHARING CHRIST

Christ requires an apostolic passion. For the apostles, Jesus Christ was the good news. This conviction is the only power that will give us the passion to be for our age what the first-century Christians were for theirs. What we believe about what Christ can do for persons will determine how we order our life as disciples and the life of the Christian community of which we are a part.

It is exciting, yet daunting, to know that our marching orders are so expansive and demanding—to share the gospel with the whole world. Jesus knew we would tremble at such a thought, so he gave us his promise, "I am with you always, to end of the age" (Matt. 28:20). Here is the added promise to his earlier one, that when he "went away," he would send the Holy Spirit. And what would the Holy Spirit do? He would empower you to live as you need to live as a Christian. "You will receive power when the Holy Spirit has come upon you" (Acts 1:8).

The Christian community is to be Spirit-empowered, where love and mutual caring, forgiveness, healing, reconciliation, restoration, deliverance, social witness, and the breaking down of racial, economic, and social barriers are anticipated as the norm—not the miraculous.

The Great Commission and the Holy Spirit go together. We cannot obey the Great Commission effectively without the power and the presence of the Holy Spirit. But also, if we are following the Spirit's leading, we will be engaging in the Great Commission—not just talking about it; doing it. Michael Green has noted this bond as a hallmark of the New Testament church and a sign of poverty in the experience of the church today. He asks penetrating questions:

> Could it be that we know so little of the Spirit in any powerful way because we care so little for evangelism? Equally, that we know so little of evangelism in any powerful way because we know so little of the Spirit? These two God has joined together, and we cannot put them asunder. No evangelism, no Holy Spirit; no Holy Spirit, no evangelism. There is a vital link between them; and that explains a good deal of the powerlessness in the modern church. (*New Testament Evangelism: Lessons for Today* [Manila, OMF Publishers, 1982], pp. 136-37).

Frankly, sharing Christ seems to be difficult, and evangelism seems to evoke too many negative images for many people, perhaps even you. Yet you probably know Christ because someone loved you enough to share Christ with you. Do you love enough to share Christ with others?

QUESTIONS FOR REFLECTION

In what way and to what degree are you practicing disciplines that will transform you into the likeness of Christ? How can you share the good news with your family, your friends, your co-workers, people at church? What needs to happen in your life and in your congregation to reflect apostolic passion?

11

WHO NEEDS A DOCTOR?

ISAIAH 57:14-22; MARK 2:13-17

It's a beautiful picture. Levi was so excited. His conversion gave him a love and concern he never had before. He wanted to celebrate that. But not only that, he invited persons whom he wanted to introduce to Jesus to celebrate with him. He had a desire for them to experience what he had experienced. Have you ever had any sort of religious experience that was worth celebrating, that caused you to want to throw a party? Maybe you can deal with it better if I ask you, "How do you celebrate your religious experiences?" or "Is celebration a part of your spiritual expression?"

CELEBRATION TIME

One of my favorite hymns of modern times is "The Lord of the Dance." It is one of the less-traditional hymns in present-day hymnals. I like it not only because of its message but also because it is set to the tune of the American Shaker hymn "Tis a Gift to Be Simple." That's a creative connection because the Shakers used to dance in their worship.

In the mid-1960s, I wrote my most autobiographical book, entitled *Dancing at My Funeral.* One of my contentions was, and still is, that our real test in facing life is whether we run, fight, whimper, or dance. Though I am a very poor dancer, the dance became a metaphor of the Christian life for me. I was so pleased that Sydney Carter wrote "The Lord of the Dance" about the same time that my book was being published. I'm more than pleased that the hymn was finally included in the official *United Methodist Hymnal* in 1988.

"The Lord of the Dance" declares that the proper response on learning the meaning of the gospel is to celebrate—to dance. Have you ever noted how much of the gospel has to do with parties and celebrations? When the prodigal son came home, the father wanted to celebrate, so he threw a great party. When the woman who had lost her coin found it, she invited her neighbors to come in and celebrate with her. When the shepherd went out into the wilderness to find the one lost sheep, on finding that sheep and returning home, he shouted out to his neighbors that he had found the sheep that was lost and then he invited them to celebrate with him.

There's a great deal of celebration in the Scripture. In fact, according to the Book of Revelation, when Christ comes again and history is drawn to a close, there is going to be a great marriage feast in the Kingdom. Christ the Groom,

The Grace-Filled Life

and his Bride, the church, will be united; and we will all sit at the banquet table of joy and celebration.

So Levi had a party. Jesus and his disciples were there, along with "many tax collectors and sinners" (Mark 2:15). But not everyone was happy. The Pharisees didn't like it. That's what the third verse of "The Lord of the Dance" talks about. "I danced on the Sabbath when I cured the lame; / the holy people said it was a shame." Jesus' behavior was shameful in the eyes of what the hymn writer calls the "holy people." "Holy people"—the Pharisees—believed that religion should be more like mourning rather than dancing, about judgment rather than celebration, about fasting rather than feasting.

Levi—or Matthew, which would become his Christian name—was a tax collector. This meant that he was disreputable because he worked for the Romans, and therefore was an outcast in the Jewish community. Jesus not only associated with him but called him to be a disciple. The text indicates that Jesus tells Matthew to gather all his tax collector and sinner friends together, and he will eat with the whole bunch of them. The Pharisees were shocked. They asked, "Why does he eat with tax collectors and sinners?" (2:16). Jesus overhears their comments, and answers, "Those who are well have no need of a physician, but those who are sick; I have come to call not the righteous but sinners" (2:17).

SEEKING YOUR REWARD

Our suggested reading from Isaiah balances God's judgment with the promise that those who are contrite and humble will receive God's blessing, healing, comfort, and peace.

> I have seen their ways, but I will heal them;
>   I will lead them and repay them with comfort,
>   creating for their mourners the fruit of the lips.
> Peace, peace, to the far and the near, says the LORD;
>   and I will heal them. (Isa. 57:18-19)

After this announcement of "peace, to the far and the near," in chapter 58 Isaiah condemns his own people, the "righteous" ones, for their hypocritical worship and their fasting on the Sabbath in disobedience to the commands of the covenant for justice and righteousness. These earlier "righteous" ones were not far from the scribes and the Pharisees Jesus addressed. They assumed they would be recognized and rewarded for the wonderful lives they were living. They also expected God to punish the tax collectors and the sinners for the kind of life they lived. No wonder they were flabbergasted by Jesus' association with Levi and all his sinner friends.

Levi's experience invites a second question. Has a person been genuinely converted by the Grace of Christ if he does not in consequence have a desire that others be converted also? Not only was Levi celebrating the fact that he was converted, he was using that occasion to bring people together in order that they might also meet Jesus. Think about it. How deep is your desire for others to experience what you have experienced in Jesus Christ? If that desire is not deep, and if you're not doing anything about it, you might follow up with other questions: How real is my experience with Christ? Do I feel the depths of forgiveness to a point that I want to share the possibility of that forgiveness with others?

The Pharisees murmured against Jesus and his disciples because they were attending Levi's party. That raises questions about how we practice our faith, and how the faith is transferred, communicated, one to the other. Could it be that Levi gathered his tax collector friends together to meet Jesus because he knew they also wanted to leave the life they were living, a life of bondage, and be freed for the fullness of life? Isn't it true that the way we may lead people to change is by not condemning them? That is at least a part of what Jesus means when he says, "I have come to call not the righteous but sinners."

It's interesting that Jesus' call of Levi and this encounter with the Pharisees is in the setting of Mark's Gospel where he talks about Jesus' healing ministry. He tells two healing stories. In Mark 1 he tells the story of the healing of a leper. It's one of the most beautiful stories in the Scripture. A man full of leprosy—that most awful of all diseases in New Testament times—saw Jesus and fell on his knees and said to him, "If you choose, you can make me clean" (v. 40). Immediately Jesus stretched out his hands and touched the leper. I like that. He didn't keep his distance from the leper. In fact, he laid his hands upon him, and said, "I will—I will heal you—be clean." And immediately the fellow was made well.

The second story is of the lame man who was lowered through the ceiling into the presence of Jesus in order that he might be healed. The lame man had some friends who believed in the healing power of Jesus. So they took their friend to Jesus. Jesus was teaching in a house, and the house was full of people, and they couldn't get anywhere near. With the ingenuity that an ardent faith can give, those men literally tore a hole through the ceiling and lowered the man into Jesus' presence. Amazed at their remarkable faith, Jesus healed the paralytic.

With all this healing happening, it was natural for Jesus to use the image of a doctor in response to the Pharisees' criticism about eating with sinners. "Those who are well have no need of a physician." That focuses the issue. Wouldn't it be strange if a doctor thought that he was doing all he could in his work against disease if he lectured the healthy on the dangers of disease, without ever going near the sick?

The Grace-Filled Life

Two things are clear here. One, the gospel will never make it into the world with its transforming power if we Christians are afraid of getting contaminated. Someone has to run risk. Two, the church must never become a religious club where the saints are protected. My friend Len Sweet, one of the most creative communicators of the gospel I know, tells of an unforgettable experience he had at an Amy Grant concert at Kings Island near Cincinnati. It was in the midst of the controversy that swirled around her during the summer of 1986 for "crossing over" from gospel music into the secular market.

At the concert, Amy Grant talked about songs she was working on and how her tour was going. But then she became very quiet, and out of the silence she confessed the pain she was feeling because of the abuse and derision from her sisters and brothers in Christ. She then straightened up and spoke of her resolve not to listen to it. And then came these words (so powerful, Len said, that he wrote them down on the spot):

> Some people think I should stand in the light and give my witness. But I believe God has called me to stand in the dark, and there give off my light. I know there is danger in the dark, but God's Word has told me that I'm all right so long as I don't lose sight of the light. (Leonard I. Sweet, "Bibelot," 1990, Vol. 5, No. 3-6)

Amy Grant was making herself available to be the Word of God that comes to us wherever we are. But there is another side to this coin. Not only does the Word of God come to us where we are, the evangelistic task of the church is to go where the people are—and the witnessing task of the Christian is wherever the Christian is.

Who needs a doctor? Most of us do. And you can be sure of this: there are a number of persons in your own circle of friends who need a doctor. The question for most of us is not whether we will be called to witness and minister to the sickest of the sick but whether we will be faithful witnesses to those around us who have perhaps not yet realized that they are spiritually sick and are as surely spiritually doomed as those we quickly think are out of the mainstream of so-called righteousness.

QUESTIONS FOR REFLECTION

What can you celebrate about your life? If you were going to have a party to introduce Jesus and tell people what he had done for you, then let him talk to them, who would you invite? How would you talk to them?

12

A FOOL FARMER AND THE GRACE OF GOD

MARK 4:1-9

When Jesus began his ministry in Galilee, he first called four persons: Simon Peter and his brother, Andrew, then two brothers, James and John. His charge to them was "Follow me and I will make you become fishers of men" (Mark 1:17 RSV). That's strong and direct language—an imperative: "I will make you." The followers of Jesus have no choice; we are to be witnesses, "fishers of men."

Evangelism has not been a favored word in the church during the past four or five decades. There may be just cause for that in the manipulative practices of "popular evangelists," the narrow emphasis on personal salvation that reduces the Christian experience to a private issue, the "fundamentalist" framework that defines conversion as the acceptance of particular dogmatic doctrinal propositions, or the separation of evangelism from mission and commitment to holiness and justice. Too often, however, I'm afraid we have used causes that are removed from us as excuses to evade our vocation as witnesses.

Evangelism is the good news of God in Jesus Christ, expressed in word, deed, and sign, and lived out in the life of faithful followers of Christ. It is the effort on our part to reproduce the life of Christ that we have experienced and to introduce others to what we have experienced in Christ that they too may have the meaning and joy Christ provides.

I'm a United Methodist pastor. I have given the vows of church membership to thousands of people during more than fifty years of ministry. Until 2008, the final vow in our liturgy was "Will you be loyal to the church and uphold it with your prayers, presence, gifts, and service." At our 2008 General Conference, we added the "call to witness" as a fifth component of upholding the church. That action on the part of the leadership of the church, and that vow church members now take, is an expression of our vocation as Christians.

THE GOSPEL SOWER

Mark begins the fourth chapter of his Gospel with the first teachings of Jesus in parables. The first is the parable of the sower, which is followed by an explanation of its meaning. I can't think about evangelism, our witnessing vocation, without thinking of this parable.

The explanation is focused on the "soil." The sower sows the word. Some of the seeds fall along the path and birds fly down and pick them up, that is, Satan immediately comes and takes away the word that is sown. Other seeds fall on

The Grace-Filled Life

rocky ground. The seeds immediately take root and grow, but there is not enough soil for the roots to grow deeply. In the same way, when tribulation comes or persecution arises, people who have received the word superficially fall away. Other seeds are sown among the thorns. Jesus says these are those who hear the word, but the cares of life, the delights and riches of the world, and the pleasure in other things enter in and choke the word, and it proves unfruitful.

But there are those seeds that fall upon good soil. The ones who hear the word and accept it and bear fruit—they produce thirtyfold, sixtyfold, even one hundredfold.

It is a helpful reflection to consider what kind of soil we are for the seed of God's word. Most of us run around so fast in so many different directions that our souls get trampled down about as hard as the path in the parable. The seed of God's word never takes root because our souls are so barren. Our spiritual life goes to the birds! Again, some of us are like rocky soil. We have faith, but it lacks depth. Somewhere I heard someone say, "Deep down, I'm shallow!" How many of us could make that confession? The "thorny" soil is probably the best metaphor for most of us. There are so many distractions in our lives that the spiritual issues get choked out. At best, we are casually committed, so we go only a little way in response to the call to holiness.

While this is a parable about soil, there are lessons here that also can inform and inspire our thinking about our vocation as witnesses. I picture the sower going out in early spring, casting his seed in wild abandon. He knows that in those tiny little seeds is life itself. He knows that after a period of germination, the seed will burst open and explode with life.

David Buttrick, one-time professor of homiletics at Vanderbilt University, preached a sermon on this parable titled "A Fool Farmer and the Grace of God." He captured his audience with words like these:

> Can you imagine any farmer stupid enough to sow seed in a thorn bush, a rock pile, or right down the center stripe of an interstate highway? The parable is laughable, almost as silly as the Christian church sowing seed of the Gospel! We may not have tossed God's word into thorn bushes, but we've certainly preached good news in mighty odd places . . . from the rocky coasts of Alaska to the jungle thickets of South Africa, all over the world. And what's more we still do. (David C. Buttrick, *Pulpit Digest*, November-December, 1983, p. 57)

I think of my friend Olaf Parnaments and that tiny band of Christians working away in Estonia during the Soviet occupation, sowing seeds through pretend "birthday parties" when they could not gather in an explicitly Christian fashion. They never gave up in that rocky soil of constant surveillance and oppression. I think of Verla Pettit and a band of committed people deep in the heart of urban Memphis, sowing seeds of compassion in wild abandonment to the homeless, the down-and-outers. That's pretty rocky soil! I think of Billy Joe Jackson and his imaginative "willing workers" program in his effort to do what he calls economic evangelism.

"Rock, thorn, and highway: if there's anything sillier than sowing seed in a rock pile, it's the Christian church spreading the good news of the Gospel. You hear the parable and you think, 'What a dumb farmer!' " (Buttrick, p. 58). And that's what it looks like, but the farmer is saying to us, don't be too guarded in sowing seeds. "Sow the seed, no matter!"

THE SURPRISING HARVEST

Suggested in this wild abandon in sowing is another exciting truth present in the parable. There's going to be a harvest. That's what Jesus said. Sure, some seeds are going to fall on barren, rocky, even thorny ground, but look . . . look! Some falls on fertile soil, and what a harvest—thirtyfold, sixtyfold, even one hundredfold. You can count on it. There's going to be a harvest.

Look at what has happened in China. Mao and his revolution thought they had killed the church. There was no place for it in their "new China." Christians were sent to the countryside to work as peasants and be "re-educated." No one knew what was going on with the faith for nearly forty years. Then the news began to trickle out: thousands of Christians were practicing their faith underground. The seed of God's word was being planted at the risk of death. Death came to thousands, even tens of thousands—the price for sowing seed. More news suggested that there were more than a million underground Christians . . . no, more than 10 million . . . no, more than 50 million. Those who should know put the figure today at between 80 and 100 million.

There's going to be a harvest, so sow the seed, no matter! That's what evangelism is: sowing seed. As D. T. Niles put it, "Evangelism is one beggar telling another beggar where to find bread." That is not an impossible task.

QUESTIONS FOR REFLECTION

What kind of soil best describes you? What does God's wild abandon of sowing generous amounts of seed say about who God is? What do you believe is the primary task of your church in your community? How do you practice evangelism? In what way do you see yourself as an evangelist?

The Grace-Filled Life

13

GOD OUTWITS US

JOB 26:11-14; PSALM 37:1-11

Many know the name Brother Lawrence, the author of the classic spiritual guide *Practicing the Presence of God*. A part of his story is well-known. He served in the kitchen of his monastery and said he experienced the presence of God as clearly when he washed pots and pans as when he took Holy Communion.

Like many others, Brother Lawrence entered a monastic order believing he was giving up the world's happiness to become a monk. But there he discovered a much deeper happiness than he had ever imagined. On one occasion, when he was praying and reflecting on this turn of events, Brother Lawrence shouted to God, "You have outwitted me."

Isn't that a delightful phrase? God, you have outwitted me. What a testimony to the providence of God, the working of God's grace in our lives.

INTEGRITY INSIDE AND OUT

The providence of God is an ongoing theme of Scripture. It is expressed in powerful ways. This is what Job wrestled with. How could what he is suffering be God's design for his life? His friend, Bildad, has spoken about the impossibility of a mortal being righteous before God (Job 25), concluding that we mortals are maggots and worms. Job mocks him. "How you have helped one who has no power! How you have assisted the arm that has no strength!"(26:1-2).

Despite his suffering and the superficial teaching of his friends, Job keeps his integrity and refuses to surrender to despair. "As long as my breath is in me . . . my lips will not speak falsehood" (27:3, 4). Job teaches us that

> integrity is holding our lives together in order to be the same person inside and out. Unless we are together there is no source of power to resist the onslaught of dishonesty and corruption constantly coming our way. Losing our integrity is somewhat like losing our lungs—essential for life. If our lungs (integrity) collapse, all of life is threatened. (*Wesley Study Bible*, Life Application Topic: Integrity, p. 636)

So, after mocking Bildad, still questioning his suffering, Job sings of the greatness of God, concluding,

> "These are indeed but the outskirts of his ways;
> and how small a whisper do we hear of him!
> But the thunder of his power who can understand?" (26:14)

Even though he didn't understand, he never doubted God's providence, even exclaiming, "Though He slay me, yet will I trust Him" (13:15 NKJV). He might well exclaim with Brother Lawrence, "God, you have outwitted me!"

"COMMIT YOUR WAY TO THE LORD"

This ongoing theme of Scripture, God's providence, is expressed in powerful ways, especially in the Psalms. Psalm 37 is among numerous expressions of it. Note a portion of it.

> Trust in the LORD, and do good;
>   dwell in the land and enjoy safe pasture. . . .
> Commit your way to the LORD;
>   trust in him, and he will do this:
> He will make your righteousness shine like the dawn,
>   the justice of your cause like the noonday sun. (Psalm 37:3, 5-6 NIV)

The word *providence* comes from the same root as our word *provide*. Our God is a power greater than all the powers, and that power is baptized in love. God's providence is flavored by God's grace. So the psalmist could be confident. "Delight yourself in the LORD / and he will give you the desires of your heart" (v. 4 NIV). The apostle Paul expressed the same confidence, testifying to his commitment no matter what his circumstances were. In the midst of plenty or want, whether hungry or well fed, he affirmed, "I can do all things through him who strengthens me" (Phil. 4:13).

It is the consistent witness of Scripture: we are children of the Father; our God will provide and care for us. Here is an extra dimension of that truth: God often provides in surprising ways, making us echo Brother Lawrence, "God, you have outwitted me."

GOD OUTWITS ME

I experienced this dramatically in my "vocational journey." I accepted the presidency of Asbury Theological Seminary kicking and screaming. It was not what I wanted to do. Jerry (my wife) and I were blissfully happy, and our lives were filled with meaning. I didn't want to give up preaching to the same people Sunday after Sunday, being present as pastor in the deepest, most significant times of peoples' lives. Jerry had her own ministry—counseling and encouraging women in jail; organizing and working with Habitat for Humanity, which grew into our own congregation's ministry of providing housing for the working poor; a clown and mime troop that ministered in worship, but particularly in hospitals and nursing homes.

The congregation was growing, having reached almost 6,000 in membership. Our outreach ministry in Memphis and around the world was expanding and increasing in effectiveness. I had a unique and popular TV/radio ministry called *Perceptions* seen and heard by thousands every day. Over 60 percent of the people who joined our church visited for the first time because they heard *Perceptions*. Not only did we not want to leave our congregation, we did not want to leave our city where my twelve years as a pastor and preacher had been so rich and rewarding. And, as if that were not enough, two of our three adult children were living in Memphis. We didn't want to leave them.

For six months I struggled with the invitation of the seminary trustees to be their president. They were clear that they were being led by God. But I was far from clear. Jerry discerned the call before I did. Why could I not receive this as God's call? They were all so sure.

If this was God's call, I thought, God was asking too much. But finally it came clear. It is enough to say that I felt the move to be God's will, and I was not pleased at all. I responded reluctantly, even grudgingly. I yielded, but without excitement, anticipation, or joy. My attitude was "This is what I have to do." So I gritted my teeth and went anyway.

God outwitted me! The richness of our life in that community of learning, worship, and prayer was indescribable. Almost every week, I had the privilege of hearing the witness of some student who was passionately in love with Jesus and desirous of pleasing him. I discovered soon that I was participating in a Kingdom enterprise that was sending persons to the end of the world to live and proclaim the gospel, and to spread scriptural holiness across the land. I could not have imagined such joy and meaning as I had during those years at Asbury. And I had thought I was giving up something—sacrificing. God outwitted me!

The whole of God's relationship to us and the expression of God's life in the world is an outwitting dynamic. The Creator of all that is, the Sovereign God of the universe, has revealed himself as a loving father and comes to us in Jesus Christ who gave himself on the cross for our redemption. God outwits us not only by accepting us where we are but by not leaving us as we are. God's grace is sufficient, but God outwits us by giving us far more than we ask, think, or even imagine.

QUESTIONS FOR REFLECTION

Recall and spend some time reflecting on an occasion when God outwitted you. What are you doing in your life that you could not do without the power and love of God? If someone asked you, "How have you seen the providence of God working in your life?" what would you tell them?

14

WHAT PRICE INTEGRITY?

JOB 27:1-6; MARK 8:34-38

It happened in an African nation under a dictatorial government. All the students in the government schools were required to wear government uniforms. A young African student came from a Christian family that was seeking to live the faith in a challenging dominant culture of Islam along with ancestor worship and animist religion. He was a part of the Methodist Youth Fellowship and proudly wore the pin that was the insignia of the group. "I have decided to follow Jesus," he said, "I am a Christian, and this pin is my witness." His teacher told him it was dangerous to wear the pin because the government was demanding total loyalty and the officials would punish him for disobedience.

But he wore the pin; his mind was made up. So were the minds of the officials. They decided to make a public example of him. They put him in the center of a circle of students and demanded he take off his Christian pin. Quietly, he refused, determined to make his witness.

They beat him savagely until he was within a whisker of death. One more chance; would he give up? No way, he indicated, shaking his head. They struck another blow, and he stopped breathing. As they carried him away on a stretcher, a surprising thing happened. His sister, still in the circle, reached into her pocket, took out her Methodist Youth Fellowship emblem, and pinned it on her government uniform.

What price integrity! What price discipleship!

TOTAL FAITHFULNESS

When I think of integrity, I think of Job. He relentlessly insisted on the fact that he had not sinned, that what was happening to him was unfair if, as his friends insisted, he was suffering because of his sin. "As God lives, who has taken away my right, / and the Almighty, who has made my soul bitter" (Job 27:2), he exclaimed, telling the truth about how he felt about God. "As long as my breath is in me . . . my lips will not speak falsehood. . . . Until I die I will not put away my integrity from me" (vv. 3-5). A long look at Job teaches us that integrity is more than honesty and truth-telling. It is knowing and staying true to ourselves no matter what it costs.

> For what will it profit them to gain the whole world and forfeit their life?
> Indeed, what can they give in return for their life? (Mark 8:36-37)

Jesus' question is a probing one. We have experienced some of its cutting edge ourselves. It is possible to sacrifice principle for popularity, character for cash. Most of us have seen people sacrifice lasting things for those that are cheap and tawdry. What else is a man or woman doing when he or she violates the fidelity of marriage for an "exciting" affair that brings little more than sexual satisfaction for a season? Many politicians who could have been statesmen never become so because they sell their soul on the altar of popularity and compromise.

PAY IT FORWARD

Losing our integrity is life-threatening. The price we pay for the loss is not always a one-time payment. I don't know how or when it came, but this truth is real to me: *we usually pay for the good things of life in advance.* The athlete pays in advance to be a winner, usually through arduous, sometimes excruciating discipline. The concert pianist pays in advance for the world audience that thrills to the music—practicing hour upon hour, day after day.

Usually—not always, but usually—we pay for the good things in advance, while *our sins and failure are paid for in the installment plan.*

There is nothing more central in the gospel than forgiveness. Everything God is and everything God does—everything he did in Jesus Christ—points to forgiveness. But forgiveness does not mean that the results of our sins are annulled. Sometimes there is a diminishing of the painful and debilitating result of sin. It is as though we are given a special portion of God's grace. But most of the time the life of sin carries with it an awful, natural retribution. Our loss of integrity, the sin that we commit, the evil that we do comes back to demand a price. Often we pay that price in an installment fashion.

I can introduce you to dozens of alcoholics who would tell you their unique story of paying for a life given over to the enslavement of alcohol. I could sit you down with a dozen men who would tell you their story of spending most of their time and energy in their quest for money, professional success, material security. Some of them would tell you about the wife they lost in the process; others of the emotional loss their children experienced; and still others, the tragic tale of making it to the top but finding no meaning there.

Our sin and failure, losing our integrity, is usually paid for in installments. So Jesus asks, what good is it for a man to gain the whole world, yet forfeit his soul? Or what can a man give in exchange for his soul?

QUESTIONS FOR REFLECTION

How have you stood up for your faith? What price do you place on your friendships, marriage, children, relationship with God, health, peace? Are you still "paying" a price for sin or failure in your past?

15

Prayer Is a Hunger

PSALM 42

Prayer is at the heart of the Christian life. If not the greatest, it is certainly one of the greatest privileges given us as Christians. Before today is past you will have eaten something—probably three meals and maybe a snack between. Eating is natural and necessary. If you haven't yet eaten today, the chances are you have at least had a cup of coffee or tea, or a glass of water or milk. Drinking is natural and necessary. Like eating and drinking, prayer is not something foreign to our human nature. Prayer is perhaps the deepest impulse of the human soul.

Prayer is related to our search for meaning, our longing for relationship, and our need to grow. Prayer, however practiced, is an expression of our hunger for God. This hunger is a part of who we are. The Psalms are basically prayers—the prayers of the people of Israel. People from all walks and stations of life have found in the Psalms guidance, comfort, hope, strength in suffering, and teaching. Though most of the Psalms were used in corporate worship, they reflect the deep cries of individuals.

Though the Psalms are sources of prayer, they also teach us to pray. At any time during our journey through the Psalms, we might stop and engage in our own personal prayer inspired by the prayer experience of the psalmist, or reflect on the nature of prayer as the psalmist wrestles in honest confrontation with life situations and his experience of God. Psalm 42 begs for that kind of engagement. It moves us to prayer and teaches us about prayer, so we can use it as a launchpad for reflection on prayer.

Prayer is a hunger and nothing, absolutely nothing else can completely satisfy that hunger. It is a hunger to experience meaning, to know that life has purpose. Prayer is something deep within us calling to something deeper yet, making us restless, unsettled, even confused because we are vaguely aware that we are not being and doing what we were meant to be and do.

The psalmist spoke the truth in unforgettable language.

> As a hart longs for flowing streams,
>   so longs my soul for thee, O God.
> My soul thirsts for God, for the living God.
>   When shall I come and behold the face of God? (Ps. 42:1-2 RSV)

The psalmist poured out his soul to God—cried, even screamed, from the depths of his being. He was confident that his soul's hunger could be satisfied only by the Lord.

To affirm that prayer is a hunger—and that at the heart of it is mystery—is the place at which we must begin our praying. Otherwise we will be handling holy things with dirty and clumsy hands. However, we must go beyond this affirmation. The God who made us for himself is like Jesus, who loves us to the point that he will even die for us.

The first epistle of John provides a marvelous description of who we are in relation to God. "Consider the incredible love that the Father has shown us in allowing us to be called 'Children of God.' " And that is not just what we are called, but who we are: "Here and now, my dear friends, we are God's children. We don't know what we shall become in the future. We only know that when He appears we shall be like Him, for we shall see Him as He is!" (1 John 3:1-2 Phillips).

John had been with Jesus in the Upper Room. He had heard Jesus say,

> Greater love has no man than this, that a man lay down his life for his friends. You are my friends. . . . No longer do I call you servants, for the servant does not know what his master is doing; but I have called you friends, for all that I have heard from my Father I have made known to you. (John 15:13-15 RSV)

In the context of this understanding of a God like Jesus—who loves us and dies for us, and who wishes us to be his children who are his friends—we accept the simplest, most straightforward definition of prayer. *Prayer is fellowship with God.*

The surest sign of fellowship, and that which builds relationship, is conversation—talking and listening to another. This is happening in Psalm 42. Though the psalmist doesn't have the revelation of God in Jesus that we have, he expresses himself honestly. "I say to God, my rock, 'Why have you forgotten me?' " (v. 9). He continues to pour out his troubled soul, always asking himself the question, "Why are you cast down, O my soul" (vv. 5, 11). But he knows God's love, and he trusts him, "Hope in God; for I shall again praise him, / my help and my God" (v. 11).

Because it is natural to pray does not mean it is easy to pray. To pray consistently requires commitment and discipline. Don't condemn yourself if you find praying difficult. Most of us do—even those we call saints. Discipline is essential for a consistent life of prayer. We need to remember, however, that the purpose of discipline is to enhance and increase the spontaneous dimension of praying and, along with other spiritual disciplines, to conform us to the image of God's Son, Jesus.

WE PRAY TO EXPERIENCE GOD

One final thought: *We pray to experience God.* The first sentence of Psalm 63 is a great personal claim: "God, you are my God." The heart of prayer is communion. Communion means "being with," sharing our experience. Persons say that they don't pray because God is not real to them. A truer statement would be that God is not real to them because they do not pray. Harry Emerson Fosdick puts this graphically:

> The practice of prayer is necessary to make God not merely an idea held in the mind but a Presence recognized in the life. In an exclamation that came from the heart or personal religion, the psalmist cried, "O God, thou art my God" (Psalm 63:1). To stand afar off and say "O God" is neither difficult nor searching . . . but it is an inward and searching matter to say, "O God, thou art my God." The first is theology, the second is religion; the first involves only opinion, the second involves vital experience; the first can be reached by thought, the second must be reached by prayer; the first leaves God afar off, the second alone makes Him real. To be sure, all Christian service where we consciously ally ourselves with God's purpose, and all insight into history where we see God's providence at work help to make God real to us; but there is an inward certainty of God that can come only from personal communication with God. (Maxie Dunnam, *The Workbook of Living Prayer*, p. 30)

This may be a new thought to you—that we pray not only because God is real, but we pray for God to be more real to us.

It may be that we will never learn to pray, never have any ongoing, creatively disciplined prayer life until our desire for communion with God is so great that we will be driven to prayer. The Psalms help us as we not only study them, but as we *allow them to study us and speak to us the things of God.*

QUESTIONS FOR REFLECTION

How does your hunger for communion with God express itself? How much of your prayer time is spent simply sharing your life with God? How much more real does God need to be for you to become more kind and loving?

16

THE GOSPEL BY WHICH WE ARE SAVED

1 CORINTHIANS 15:1-11

The central fact of the Christian faith is the resurrection of Jesus Christ. Had it all ended with the Cross, there would be no good news to share, no Christian community of faith to bear bold witness.

WITHOUT THE RESURRECTION THERE IS NO CHRISTIANITY

The Apostle Paul knows that, so he writes the fifteenth chapter of his first Letter to the Corinthians. Here, Paul is the first person to record in writing what had been preached for years following Jesus' death and resurrection.

Can you imagine what it must have been like before all this was written down, to hear the unbelievable story of God coming to us in Jesus Christ: being born a baby to a virgin, growing up as a normal human being, making fantastic claims about coming from God and going to God, shocking all with his radical message of love and forgiveness, being condemned to die and willingly accepting death, forgiving those who hung him on the cross, promising to come again. And it happened. God raised him from the grave, and he was alive.

Of course, there were questions and debates. We can see them in this fifteenth chapter of 1 Corinthians. We don't know the precise question; we only know that someone was questioning the Resurrection. Paul answered the question by sharing the substance of the gospel. "I want to remind you of the gospel I preached to you. . . . By this gospel you are saved" (v. 1 NIV). Let's try to grasp the full meaning of that, "the gospel by which you are saved." Saved is a word that some are uncomfortable using. We haven't separated it from the preaching that sought to frighten us into salvation by painting the horrors of hellfire and brimstone. Often salvation is portrayed as strictly a matter of life after death with little relevance to life now. But salvation is so much more.

We must not allow a distortion or past negative experience to hinder our honestly dealing with who we are and where we are. William Law, one of the great writers about the nature of our life outside Christ and inside salvation, says,

> The reason we know so little of Jesus Christ as our Savior . . . why we are so destitute of that faith in him which alone can change, rectify, and redeem our souls, why we live starving in the coldness and deadness of a formal, historical, hearsay religion is this: we are strangers to the inward misery and wants, we know not that we are in the jaws of death and hell. (Mary Cooper Robb, ed., *The Life of*

Christian Devotion: Devotional Selections from the Works of William Law [Nashville: Abingdon, 1961], p. 135)

Sooner or later we do know, don't we? It doesn't take much reflection to acknowledge that the things we have wanted most and the things we thought would set us free have not done so. We look in the mirror and know the person there is not the person we want to be, nor are we the persons God has called us to be. And then, praise God, somehow it gets through to us: true faith is coming to Jesus Christ to be saved and delivered from our sinful nature. So Paul's word comes as a joyous certainty: "Christ died for our sins . . . was buried . . . [and] was raised . . ." (1 Cor. 15:3-4). *That's the gospel by which we are saved.*

That brings us back to where we began. The central fact of the Christian faith is the resurrection of Jesus. Had it all ended with the Cross, there would be no good news to share, no gospel by which we are saved. Paul makes that scathingly clear. "If there is no resurrection of the dead, then Christ has not been raised; . . . then our proclamation has been in vain and your faith has been in vain" (vv. 13-14).

GOD'S GIFT: NOT EARNED BUT FREELY GIVEN

For Paul, the Christ event is whole. *What gives meaning to the birth of Jesus Christ is the life of Jesus Christ.* Had he not lived a sinless life, the virgin birth would have been meaningless. *What gives meaning to the life of Jesus Christ is his death.* If he had not given his sinless life as a sacrifice for our sins, then his sinless life would have been meaningless. The climax comes in the Resurrection. *What gives meaning to the death of Jesus is the Resurrection.* If he had not been raised, then he could not have been who he said he was, and therefore his birth, life, and death would all be meaningless.

The gospel by which we are saved is Christ who is alive, and who can be alive in you and me. Alive to provide:
- Forgiveness for our sins
- Healing for our brokenness
- Direction for our lostness
- Joy for our sadness
- And, one day, our own resurrection from the dead for eternal life with him.

QUESTIONS FOR REFLECTION

Look at the five things listed above that are provided by the living Christ. Ask yourself: Have I received this gift? Why am I failing to receive it? How might I enable others to receive these gifts?

17

FRESH EVERY MORNING

EXODUS 16:1-8; PSALM 50:7-15; 2 CORINTHIANS 1:1-11

My most fruitful and rewarding experience with Scripture comes out of what I call "devotional reading." In a time of quietness, reflection, and prayer, I simply begin reading a passage of Scripture. Relaxed, with no specific effort to find some truth or support some conviction, I read until some word grabs my attention. I stay with that word, letting it tumble around in my mind. I try to hear it personally, to "taste" it by reflecting on it. I allow it to speak to my heart as well as to my mind, to tap my feelings. I ask it questions and allow it to question me. Then I form my specific prayer for that moment out of that encounter with God's word.

GOD SAYS, "CALL ON ME"

I was reading Psalm 50 in that fashion and came to verse 15: "Call on me in the day of trouble; / I will deliver you, and you shall glorify me." It's interesting that I do not recall why that verse grabbed my attention—except that I am like most people: trouble is often my lot. Maybe I was concerned about one of my children or a grandchild. Maybe I was wrestling with a decision. Maybe it was the financial crisis through which I was going or my struggle with vocational expression.

Whatever the situation, there it was. God's word offering a fantastic promise I needed: *deliverance*—not many of us pass through too many days without needing it. As I reflected on this staggering promise, I became aware of the fact that in the translation I was reading, the promise was not a complete sentence, although it was recorded as a separate verse. It began with the word *and*, so I went back to the beginning to read the complete sentence, beginning with verse 14. "Offer to God a sacrifice of thanksgiving, / and pay your vows to the Most High"—then comes the promise: "Call on me in the day of trouble; / I will deliver you."

Deliverance is connected with conditions we are to meet. The primary condition is "a sacrifice of thanksgiving," and keeping our "vows to the Most High." God is not making a wholesale promise but a promise that is to be appropriated as needed—and appropriated out of this ongoing posture of our life: dependence upon the Lord, trust in him. Give him praise and thanksgiving for what he has already done, with confidence in what he will continue to do.

Paul demonstrates this stance. He begins his Second Letter to the Corinthians by confirming the fact that though trouble and suffering may be our lot, we can count on God's everlasting arms sustaining us in our darkest hours. He calls God "the Father of mercies and the God of all consolation" (1:3). Paul shares his affliction but offers a sacrifice of praise: "Blessed be the God and Father of our Lord Jesus Christ . . . who consoles us in all our affliction" (v. 3-4).

WE FORGET SO SOON

Israel never seemed to learn this, even after they had been delivered from bondage. Their belief had a short memory. They forgot the miracle of the Red Sea within a month. They struck their timbrels and sang the "Song of Moses" (Exod. 15), thanking and praising God for their deliverance and God's triumph over Pharaoh. But look what happened.

Three days after this miraculous parting of the Red Sea and their deliverance, they came to Marah in their wilderness journey. Marah means a place of bitterness. The peoples' thirst was overwhelming, but they couldn't drink the bitter water. They raged in anger against Moses. God intervened again. He gave Moses a tree to throw into the water, and the water became sweet.

The next stop in their journey was at Elim, where there were twelve springs of water and seventy palm trees—a welcome place of rest and refreshment. Someone has suggested that God does not give us too many Elims because he can't trust us there. We grow too comfortable too fast and forget to look to God. Now and then we may rest in Elim, but we can't pitch our tent for a long season there. There will appear a cloud by day and a light by night, which is God's summons for us to move on.

Israel moved away from Elim, led by the Lord, traveling through the wilderness of Sin. Again the people showed themselves for what they were: faithless people who had not yet learned to trust the Lord. In their memory there must still have been the picture of Pharaoh's army drowned on the seashore, but now they were hungry. Though God had delivered them out of the boney hands of death, they could not believe that he could satisfy today's hunger.

They assailed Moses and Aaron with anger and began to again wish for what amounts to the grocery stores back in Egypt. They could remember and savor in their minds the security of food, shelter, and clothing they had had back in Egypt; but they had forgotten the afflictions of slavery. As many commentators have noted, *it proves easier to get the people out of Egypt than it is to get Egypt out of the people.* God intervenes again with the miracle of the manna, the bread of heaven (Exod. 16).

The miracle and one of its profound meanings is in verse 4 of Exodus 16. "Then the LORD said to Moses, 'I am going to rain bread from heaven for you, and each day the people shall go out and gather enough for that day. In that way I will test them, whether they will follow my instruction.'" The Lord was testing them. Did they really trust him? They didn't. Rather than trusting that there would be manna "fresh every morning," they sought to store it, but it "bred worms and became foul" (v. 20).

There are abundant lessons here. God is faithful; he does provide, but we cannot store up his grace. The miracle of the manna teaches us about habitual dependence upon God. God could have provided at once everything the Israelites needed for their wilderness wandering, but he didn't. He gave them only enough for the day.

Earlier, we talked about Paul's introductory word to the Corinthians, blessing God whom he called "the Father of mercies." He shared with them the afflictions he had suffered, coming to the point where he and his friends were "so utterly, unbearably crushed that we despaired of life itself." Then he made this amazing statement, "Indeed, we felt that we had received the sentence of death so that we would rely not on ourselves but on God who raises the dead" (2 Cor. 1:8, 9).

That's what God was trying to teach the Israelites—a habitual dependence upon him. The happiest people I know are not people who don't have needs but people who live by faith that their needs are going to be met by God.

FREELY GIVEN TO BE FREELY SHARED

The miracle of the manna also teaches us that there are some things we cannot store up for tomorrow. Yesterday's manna cannot be used as food for today; it cannot be hoarded.

We could catalogue a number of things that cannot be gathered in advance and stored up for tomorrow: love in the family, the sense of being accepted and forgiven by God, democracy, education, character, and even culture and civilization are tenuous. All must be attended to daily.

Overarching it all, the Christian faith is a "daily manna" issue. We can't depend on an experience we have today being repeated tomorrow unless we cultivate its meaning. We can't pray enough today to last for the week. The forgiveness we receive for sin committed today does not cover the sins we may commit next month. God's presence is appropriated daily through prayer, Scripture, worship, sharing with friends, and those spiritual disciplines that become channels through which he makes himself known.

What kinds of assurance do you need from God today? In the Lord's Prayer we ask for "our daily bread." What do you daily seek from God? What in your life reflects the fact that you don't really believe God's provision will be adequate every day? What in your life reflects you do believe his provisions will be adequate?

18

Being the Lord's Instrument

EXODUS 17:1-7; 2 SAMUEL 7:1-17

It's a terrible thing to believe that nobody needs you—that you have been put on the shelf, and all that is left now is for you to just sit there, to be present but not to count for anything. It's also a terrible thing to believe that you have lost your influence.

WHEN GOD SPEAKS, DO YOU LISTEN?

Moses was plagued with those issues throughout the Exodus journey. Over and over again, the Israelites challenged his leadership. It was no different when they arrived at Rephidim (Exod. 17). There was no water, and the people were famished. It didn't help that Moses put the whole matter in the perspective of their faith journey, asking, "Why do you test the LORD?"

We do it, don't we? We test the Lord, wanting him to prove himself over and over again. We are not content with the "big picture" of God's grace and intervention in our life; we want him to move down to the minute details of our living, proving himself repeatedly.

Moses couldn't persuade the people to think about God, to remember his mercy and leadership in the past. The people could not see God, but Moses was highly visible, so they took out their anger against him. "Why did you bring us out of Egypt, to kill us and our children and livestock with thirst?" Moses did what we would have done. He cried out to the Lord. "What shall I do with this people? They are almost ready to stone me."

Here at Rephidim is one of the lessons underscored not only throughout the Exodus journey but throughout the entire biblical story: *we are the Lord's instrument*. In response to Moses' desperate cry, the Lord answered, "Go on ahead of the people . . . take in your hand the staff with which you struck the Nile, and go. I will be standing there in front of you on the rock at Horeb. Strike the rock, and water will come out of it, so that the people may drink" (vv. 5-6).

WHAT IS IN YOUR HAND?

Moses' rod was used by God through Moses throughout the wilderness wandering: to turn the Nile into blood, to separate the Red Sea, and now to bring water from a rock. It's a powerful image: every person has some capacity. And to all of us God is asking what he asked Moses years earlier, when he called him to deliver Israel from bondage: "What is that in your hand?" (Exod. 4:2).

Reading Scripture, *we realize that God takes for granted that each of us has something that is useful for him and his ministry.* While there may not be equality of gifts and talent, every person has intrinsic worth in God's kingdom. Our usefulness to God is not measured by the character or capacity of our gifts but by our willingness to use those gifts for God.

OUR GIFTS BUT GOD'S WAY

To be sure, we have to be diligent in discerning God's call and how he intends us to use the gifts he has given us. Chapter seven of 2 Samuel tells the story of David running ahead of God's call, even mishearing it. David has ascended to the throne of Israel, is established in his own "new house." Perhaps he is preoccupied with himself and his own insecurities. He has not yet proved himself as king, so he focuses on himself and decides that he must build God a house. In his own mind God has already said yes to his idea.

When David has said yes, in himself, he decides that he will consult Nathan the Prophet. It is a common ego-support move we often make. We make up our minds what we are going to do, and then we seek "counsel" to confirm and authenticate what we have already decided. Nathan is thrilled and excited that such a distinguished person, the King of Israel, would seek his advice. It doesn't matter who we are—prophet, priest, pastor, friend—*we must be careful that we are not so flattered by someone seeking our guidance that we too easily confirm what we know they desire.*

David reveals to Nathan his thoughts concerning the building of the Temple. Nathan is enthusiastic. No wonder Nathan is excited; prophets aren't accustomed to kings offering to do something for God. Without seeking guidance himself, Nathan tells David to "go for it," giving David the green light to go ahead with his dream to build a house for God. But that night Nathan heard from God. God didn't see David's intention in the same light that Nathan did. Early the next morning Nathan went to the king and revoked his building permit.

On the surface, David's motive seems right. "See now," he said to Nathan, "I am living in a house of cedar, but the ark of God stays in a tent" (7:2). But God knew. David, though later described as a "man after God's own heart," *was full of himself*, not following God. We have to be careful, and we have to have godly counsel when we are seeking to be the Lord's instrument.

The message from Nathan to David is blunt, forthright, and final. David was not to build God's house; God was going to build David a house. The prophet rehearses for David the Lord's work in his life: "I took you from the pasture, from following the sheep to be prince over my people Israel" (v. 8). God was going to use David as his instrument but not always in the way David would have it.

WE ARE INSTRUMENTS WITH UNIQUE VOICES

To be the Lord's instrument, *we must keep a sense of our own uniqueness*. There are no carbon copies in God's family.

In her beautiful and moving autobiography *I Know Why the Caged Bird Sings*, Maya Angelou talks about growing up in the South. She celebrates the uniqueness of the unrepeatable miracle of God each one of us is, dedicating the book to her son, "Guy Johnson, and all the strong blackbirds of promise who defy the odds and gods and sing their song." That's a beautiful expression of keeping a sense of our own uniqueness, which is necessary if we are to be the Lord's instrument.

Knowing that *no matter who we are, where we are, and the nature of our gifts we can be useful* is a second essential for being the Lord's instrument. I'm not the marching kind, but one march I will always remember. The World Methodist Council was meeting in Dublin, Ireland. To show our solidarity with the women of the Republic of Ireland who were supporting the women of Northern Ireland, some of us joined their march demonstrating for peace in that ravaged land.

The Women's Peace Movement began in Northern Ireland. On August 10, 1976, an IRA gang of terrorists made a strike on a city and were speeding away in their car when British troops opened fire. They hit the driver of the car. The car careened out of control and killed three children of the McGuire family.

The next day, August 11, a young housewife named Betty Williams stood up and said, "I've had enough." She got TV and press coverage with a message that it was time the violence between Catholics and Protestants that was tearing their beautiful land apart and destroying human life had to end. She asked all who wanted to do something about it to attend a rally on August 14, which was the day following the burial of the three McGuire children.

That day will long be remembered in Ireland. For the first time in Northern Ireland, Roman Catholics and Protestants came together and the Irish Women for Peace was organized through Betty Williams, a Protestant, and Mairead Corrigan, a Roman Catholic.

In an interview, Betty Williams said, "There's no use sitting here and saying I believe in God and I believe in peace. You have to go out and do something about it. You have to get others to believe in God and believe in peace."

QUESTIONS FOR REFLECTION

Can you recall an occasion during the past year when you were used as the Lord's instrument? What gifts do you bring to God's kingdom? Do you have the gift of patience, peace-making, money-making, mercy, justice, discernment, beauty, music, teaching? How are you using these gifts?

19

FIRST THEY GAVE THEMSELVES TO THE LORD

2 CORINTHIANS 8:1-15

Paul is involved in collecting money for the needy Christians in Jerusalem. This collection had been going on for at least a year but had been interrupted in Corinth by the confusion and conflict among the Christians there, as well as their disfavor with Paul. Reconciliation has taken place, the church is now centered again, and Paul calls on them to complete what they had started earlier.

REPENT AND RESOLVE

Reconciliation has taken place because the church in Corinth has repented. Ponder that for a moment. We usually think of repentance that results in conversion, when we acknowledge sorrow for sin, accept the forgiveness of Christ, and resolve to sin no more. But *repentance is no one-time thing*. The resolve to sin no more must be a lifelong pattern that is active through the power of the Holy Spirit.

In Paul's expression of his personal relief at the reconciliation he now has with the Christians in Corinth, he provides direction for our ongoing repentance as Christians. "Now I rejoice, not because you were grieved, but because your grief led to repentance; for you felt a godly grief, so that you were not harmed in any way by us. For godly . . . repentance . . . leads to salvation and brings no regret, but worldly grief produces death" (2 Cor. 7:9-10).

GIVING LIBERALLY AND SACRIFICIALLY

Now that reconciliation has taken place, the church can resume and complete the collection that would deepen their Christian life. It would expand their horizons and help bind Gentile and Jewish Christians in fellowship. Perhaps overarching everything else, the Corinthians needed to learn the blessing that comes from generosity.

To accomplish this with the Corinthians, Paul tells of some other Christians in Macedonia. Macedonia was an economically depressed area. These Christians were as poor as the Christians in Jerusalem for whom the offering was being taken. Yet when Paul announces the need of the suffering Christians in Jerusalem, the way the Macedonians responded is a guide for the living and giving of all Christians. "They . . . gave according to their means, and even beyond their means" (8:3). But here is the shocking word: "Begging us earnestly for the privelege of sharing in this ministry to the saints" (v. 4).

That's the kind of church God wants: a church of people with generous hearts who gladly return God's tithes—ten percent of their income—as a natural act because they know that's the minimum God requires. *To give liberally out of a generous heart is the pattern of the Christian.*

The Macedonians not only gave liberally out of a generous heart, *they gave sacrificially.* Chapter 8 begins with some surprising words. "We want you to know, brothers and sisters, about the grace of God that has been granted to the churches of Macedonia; for during a severe ordeal of affliction, their abundant joy and their extreme poverty have overflowed in a wealth of generosity on their part" (v. 1-2). These Christians had suffered persecution for their faith; and in addition, they were poverty-stricken. Yet the test of affliction resulted in an abundance of joy, and their poverty overflowed in a wealth of liberality.

JOY FROM SACRIFICE

It's not an everyday occurrence, but I have seen hardship and sacrifice release a fountain of joy, persons in the midst of their suffering coming alive in the depth of faith. As a pastor, I saw and heard it often. Here are a few examples.

From a person who has been without work for six months: "I know now what it means to trust the Lord. Though I'm not on the brink of poverty, I have a faint taste of what people must feel who have to scratch out a living day in and day out."

From a young man whose wife died, leaving him with a seven-year-old to rear alone: "Her faith was so vibrant and alive," he said. "The way she died is teaching me how to live."

When we see it, we rejoice: the possibility that affliction and suffering can result in an abundance of joy.

At first glance we may think the description of the Macedonians has nothing to do with us. "Their extreme poverty . . . overflowed in a wealth of generosity" (v. 2). It has everything to do with us because it describes more than their sacrificial giving; it designates their real wealth. *Their wealth was in their love that expressed itself in generosity.* We have a generous God. When we are generous, we reflect God in the world.

As I travel the world, as I seek to observe and read and reflect, I see two ways in which the world is being destroyed: *outward poverty* and *inward emptiness.* The first, outward poverty, is painfully obvious. We could recite the statistics—963 million people go hungry every day in developing countries and 11 million children die every year from preventable and treatable diseases. Hunger and malnutrition contribute to 60 percent of these deaths. In the

United States, 12.6 million children live in households where people have to skip meals or eat less to make ends meet. Thousands of children will be born today without a chance to live beyond one year because there will be no adequate nourishment for them. Disease-ridden ghettoes in cities around the world make life a nightmare because of poverty.

Christ came into the world so that all might have life in all its fullness, yet an absolute impoverishment is destroying people not only physically and mentally but also spiritually. What comes between Christ and the world's impoverished peoples is exploitation, the sin of the "haves" who, maybe without intention, prevent the fulfillment of Christ's promise.

Not only outward poverty but also inward emptiness is destroying our world. The plight of the so-called "third world" is outward poverty. The plight of our world, the so-called "first world" is inward emptiness. That's the reason this text has meaning to the middle class, the upper-middle class, and the wealthy. "Their extreme poverty overflowed in a wealth of generosity." As a rule, poorer people give a greater percentage of their income than wealthy people. Does this mean that poorer people are more generous? Do the poor reflect God better than the rich?

THE LOVE WE SHOW

Our wealth does not only consist in what we have but in who we know ourselves to be and the inner resources we have cultivated in our relationship to Christ. Narrowing that focus, *a person's wealth consists not alone in what he has, but in the love he shows*. We're rich or poor according to the depth of our compassion. Paul makes this clear when he compares the grace of God working in the Macedonians with the grace of Jesus Christ. "For you know the [grace] of our Lord Jesus Christ, that though he was rich, yet for your sakes he became poor, so that by his poverty you might become rich" (v. 9).

The key to it all was the personal commitment of the Macedonians. Paul describes it. "They gave themselves first to the Lord" (v. 5). This is the giving that counts for eternity—in fact, when we give ourselves in this fashion, we secure all of our tomorrows with God.

Alan Paton once said the key question for a Christian is not "Am I saved?" but "Am I giving?" I'm not sure I would put it just that way, but there's no question about it—if you want to test your salvation, test your generosity. If you are not growing in your generosity—not just of your money but also of your time and talent, of your whole self—then you might well question your Christian experience.

The model for our generosity is the greatest challenge. We give because Christ has given to us. If we are rich in the way that really matters, the material riches that we possess will be seen as a gift of God and used for his glory.

QUESTIONS FOR REFLECTION

Would those who know you describe you as a generous person? How do you see the destructive power of inward impoverishment at work?

20

THE ARK: GOD'S SAVING AND
EMPOWERING PRESENCE

GENESIS 6:5-8; EXODUS 25:10-22; JOSHUA 3:2-6

There are many arks mentioned in the Bible—all saving arks. The first is Noah's ark, an ark of promise, a saving ark. The beginning of the story is in Genesis 6. The wickedness of humanity "was great in the earth," so disappointing and revolting to God that he was "sorry that he had made humankind . . . and it grieved him to his heart" (v. 6). But Noah found favor "in the sight of the LORD" (v. 8), and the Lord decided to use him as the saving remnant of humankind.

SAVED BY GOD'S ARKS

The Lord commanded Noah to build the ark. Risking the ridicule of his neighbors, Noah began to build a huge boat on dry land with no water in sight. Just as he finished, the heavens opened and rain fell for forty days and nights. Humankind was saved by Noah's ark of faithfulness.

A long time after Noah, Moses' mother, knowing that Pharaoh had commanded that all male children be killed, did a bold and brave thing. Immediately after Moses was born, she risked everything by hiding him away for three months. When he was too old to hide, she built a little hemp boat, placed her baby within it and carried it to the riverside, laid it in a thicket of reeds, and waited for God to act. The little boat was a saving ark, keeping the infant child safe until he was rescued by the daughter of Pharaoh.

Then there was the Ark of the Covenant. It was the most important piece of furniture in the tabernacle and in Israel's history. In fact, when God gave instructions to Moses concerning the building of the tabernacle, he began with the ark. It was first, because it was first in importance. The purpose of the ark was to contain the tablets of the law, "the testimony." But more than that, it represented the presence of God in a very special way. See this idea demonstrated in three different ways in two settings.

GOD PREPARES A WAY FOR YOU

The first setting is at the River Jordan, where we witness God's *prevenient presence*. When the tabernacle was in a place, the ark was always in the "holy of holies." It was there, in the holy of holies, with the mercy seat covering the ark, that the high priest would take the blood of sacrificed lambs and pour it on the mercy seat on the Day of Atonement as a sacrifice for the sins of the people.

But the tabernacle was not always in one place, because Israel was a wandering people. Wherever they went, they would take the Ark with them. One of the thrilling accounts of God's presence through the Ark was when Joshua was leading Israel in possessing the Promised Land (Josh. 3).

The story is not quite but almost as dramatic as the crossing of the Red Sea. When the priests who bore the ark came to the Jordan, it was overflowing its banks. The overflowing river stretching before them, the Ark of the Covenant being borne by them, the call of God to "go" burning in their minds—they didn't stop. "While all Israel were crossing over on dry ground, the priests who bore the ark of the covenant of the LORD stood on dry ground in the middle of the Jordan, until the entire nation finished crossing over the Jordan" (Josh. 3:17).

It's a picture of what John Wesley called "prevenient grace," the presence of God going before us. How much psychic and emotional energy is wasted worrying about coming to places we've not been before. How often have we worried about things that never happened? Mark Twain spoke for many of us: "I'm an old man, and I've seen a lot of troubles in my lifetime that never happened."

> Do you ever ask what you will do at the swellings of Jordan? Do you fear that heart and strength will fail? Do you dread the touch of the cold water? Do you wish that you'd lived in days when bushes burned with fire, when voices spoke from the mount, when the angels seemed visible to precede the hosts . . . and one like the Son of Man walking the glowing embers with faithful witnesses? There's no need to cherish such backward yearnings. There is a presence with us—a divine companionship, the angel of the covenant, the Christ of God! Like a voice ringing down a mountain ravine, we hear his imperishable words, "Lo, I am with you all the days, even unto the end." Shall we have the faith to answer, "Yea, though I walk through the valley of the Shadow of death; I will fear no evil for thou art with me"? (F. B. Meyer, *Studies in Exodus* [London: Marshall, Morgan & Scott, 1952], p. 3030)

Even if our emotions have not yet realized the experience, will we claim it in faith—that God goes before us preveniently, preparing the way? He will meet us at every overflowing Jordan, every swelling river of our life.

GOD WILL EMPOWER YOU

Then there was the Ark at Jericho: *God's powerful presence.* What do we know of the story of Joshua at Jericho? That Jericho was a stronghold protected by mighty men and Israel was no equal to the army there, so how could they go against that city? That the strategy of Joshua for taking the city was strange indeed: all of Israel's men of war marching around the city once a day for six

The Grace-Filled Life

days, then on the seventh day, marching around the city seven times? That seven priests blowing trumpets of rams' horns followed the army.

All strange, but stranger yet, on the seventh time around the city, when the priests made a long blast on the rams' horns, all the people were to shout and the walls of the city would crumble.

That's what we know, and of course, we know the walls came a tumblin' down. What many may not know or remember about the story involves the Ark of the Covenant. In the procession around the city, each of the six days and seven times on the seventh day, the priests carrying the Ark of the Covenant followed the priests blowing the trumpets. That's the key—not the army showing their strength, not the presence of the priests and the blowing trumpets, not the commitment of those wandering people and their shout of oneness—but the Ark, the powerful presence of God.

God's presence is power. For those who abide in the secret place of the Lord, mountains and hills of fear and discouragement and sickness and pain are made low; walls of estrangement and separation and loneliness and despair come tumbling down.

Here it is in the witness of the missionary statesman Leonard T. Wolcott, as he described a person in a leprosarium.

> The man looked old, but who can tell the age of a leper? His fingers were gone from the knuckles. His nose was eaten off. Teeth hung loose in his jaw, but his eyes were very alive. I looked at him with pity. "Isn't that hard?" I asked him. He smiled and said enthusiastically: "Christ is a wonderful savior!" He was hoeing in his garden at the leprosarium, holding the hoe clumsily in his fingerless hands. Nearby a younger man, new to the leprosarium I guess, was struggling with a big weed in his own garden patch. The old man leaned over and between his paws jerked out the weed. Then he showed the younger leper how to jerk reluctant weeds. Under the hot sun I saw him tremble with the exertion. But the younger smiled his thanks and the older beamed his pleasure. "Isn't life hard?" I asked him. He smiled and shook his head: "Our Lord God is so wonderful." (*Alive Now*, September-October, 1982, p. 57)

That witness is dramatic, far removed from our daily experience, but I share it precisely for that purpose—to make the point that God's presence is power. I invite you: stay alive to that presence. Power not your own will be yours if you will stay alive to God's presence. The Ark of the Covenant at the Jordan and Jericho witness to it.

QUESTIONS FOR REFLECTION

Recall a personal experience of God's prevenient presence—God going before you. Recall a personal experience of being empowered by God. Where do you need God to heal you, guide you, forgive you, sustain you?

21

TAUGHT BY A GOLDEN CALF

EXODUS 32:1-14; LUKE 6:1-11

About six weeks preceding making and worshiping a golden calf, the people of Israel had sworn, "Everything that the LORD has spoken we will do" (Exod. 19:8). The blood of the covenant that had been sprinkled on them was scarcely dry when they cast that covenant aside and flung off their allegiance to Jehovah. They grew weary of waiting for Moses to come down from Sinai, and, not knowing what he might come back saying and doing, they prevailed upon Aaron to make "gods . . . who shall go before us" (32: 1).

IDOL WORSHIP

We think too little of idolatry. When we think about it, we picture people who carve wood or stone images and ignorantly bow down to those images. We may think of, and even be fascinated by, our experience in another country where we have seen people bringing food and flowers to a bronze Buddha, or burning incense at the feet of one of a hundred gods in a pagoda temple.

That may be idolatry as surely as the making of a golden calf, but know this: the idolater is not the only one who has never known God. Paul began his Letter to the Romans by acknowledging this fact. "For though they knew God, they did not honor him as God or give thanks to him, but they became futile in their thinking, and their senseless minds were darkened" (Rom. 1:21).

The people in our Exodus story knew God. They had seen his blazing glory and had been guided by a cloud by day and a fire by night. They had been miraculously fed manna, coming down from heaven, fresh every morning. They had heard his voice on Sinai, yet they made the calf. So an idolater is not one who has not known God but one who, having known God, refuses to glorify him or devises some substitute in life for the praise and glory and worship that belong to God.

The test is this: *whenever anyone or anything usurps the place God should have in our lives, we're guilty of idolatry.* For most of us that would not be a "graven image," but we do have our "golden calves." Some obvious ones make the point. Is one of these your "golden calf"?

MONEY. Tithing is not commanded by God as a practice to support the church and ministry. It is a spiritual discipline to remind us of how easy it is to turn money into a golden calf, to allow money—how we get it and how we use it—to edge God out of the center of our life.

SECURITY. Our neurotic drivenness for security can become a golden calf, betraying our lack of faith in God. This preoccupation with security makes people sick, tearing them to pieces emotionally. Do we believe the beautiful and heartbreaking lesson of Matthew 6:26: "Look at the birds of the air; they neither sow nor reap nor gather into barns, and yet your heavenly Father feeds them. Are you not of more value than they?"

On a national and international level, this is a big part of what the nuclear arms race is about. In the past fifty years, both Russia and the United States have made an idol of power. Both nations have enough warheads and bombs to destroy the whole world. Isn't it ironic that now our nation's biggest concerns are whether Iran or some rogue group is developing nuclear bombs or other weapons of mass destruction?

DISTORTED RELATIONSHIPS. Some subtle idolatry calls us to probe deeper. I've seen love in marriage distorted to the point that it usurps God's place in our lives. I've seen love of country corrupted to the point that it blinds people to sinful, dehumanizing practices of torture that dull us to the call to justice and righteousness. Ongoing self-examination is essential as we seek to remember that anyone or anything that usurps the place God should have in our lives is idolatry.

DISTORTED RELIGION. Come at it from a different perspective, turning something that is holy, designed for spiritual discipline and nurture, into a rigid rule that stifles Kingdom attitudes and actions. Jesus confronted this idolatry head-on. Luke records two stories of Jesus' conflicts with some of the scribes and Pharisees (Luke 6:1-11). Both stories are about Jesus' opponents becoming angry because of human need being met on the Sabbath.

Some of these scribes and Pharisees obviously had religious rules committed perfectly to memory. One of them had heard of Jesus plucking grain and eating it with his disciples on the Sabbath. The law forbade work on the Sabbath: thirty-nine specific activities were forbidden. Interestingly, plucking grain in a neighbor's field was not considered theft. Hungry passersby could satisfy their needs, even without permission of the owner. But the law forbade harvesting and threshing on the Sabbath. So Jesus and his followers, who had picked a little grain to eat, were being indicted for harvesting and threshing.

The second incident was at the scene and heart of their religious tradition— the synagogue—and the time was the Sabbath day. Jesus had entered the synagogue to teach when he came upon a man whose right hand was withered. We are told he had been a stonemason who for some time now had been forced to beg as a result of this affliction.

The scribes and Pharisees were watching every move Jesus made, so he knew their intent. He called the man to him, faced them squarely, and asked, "Is it lawful to do good or to do harm on the sabbath, to save life or to destroy it?"

Not waiting for an answer nor expecting one, he asked the man to stretch out his hand, and it was healed. A need had been met, a man had been healed, but the Pharisees "were filled with fury and discussed with one another what they might do to Jesus" (vv. 9, 11).

Jesus' teaching was clear: "The Son of Man is lord of the sabbath" (v. 5). Again, we have the golden calf issue. The scribes and Pharisees had made the Sabbath an idol, turning something that is holy, designed for spiritual discipline and nurture, into a rigid rule that stifles Kingdom attitudes and actions.

TRADITION. We know that traditions, rules, and laws are essential, giving us a necessary sense of order, structure, and continuity. Without them we could be like leaves blowing aimlessly in a wind. Christ reminds us, however, that we can distort their purpose, even use them to divert us from the primary call of the gospel: to love and serve God and neighbor as the first priority of life.

I have a friend, an ordained minister, whose life and ministry was shaped by this distortion. One Sunday afternoon, two dirty, poorly dressed boys were sitting on the well-kept grounds of the beautiful church where he was serving as a youth minister. The pastor noticed them and instructed my friend to get the boys away from the church. He did not want them there; too many church members were complaining about the "wrong kind of people" being in "our church."

My friend, then in his first years of ministry, resigned his job, knowing far better than the "senior" minister that something was wrong with that congregation's understanding of who they were and the nature of their calling as a Christian community. Since that time, my friend has devoted himself almost exclusively to serving the "least and the last."

Let's learn from the golden calf and Jesus' teaching about the Sabbath. God is sovereign Lord, and we "shall have no other gods before [him]" (Exod. 20:3). The Sabbath is holy, but holiness has most to do with our attitudes and how we live in relation to others.

QUESTIONS FOR REFLECTION

What are two things in your life that come close to being "idols"? Look at your five top priorities. Is there a "golden calf" among them?

22

THE PROOF IS IN THE PUDDING

LUKE 7:18-30

Not many people paid any attention to how John the Baptist responded to Jesus. Luke did. He recorded an event in that relationship on which a great truth about Jesus and a great truth about life hinge. John sent his disciples to inquire whether Jesus was indeed the Messiah. John had proclaimed Jesus the Messiah long before. So we wonder what's going on here.

John is in prison, soon to be executed. The kind of works that Jesus was doing didn't seem to fill the role of the Messiah as John had conceived it and as some of the prophets had talked about it. Where was the winnowing fan, the ax laid on the roots of the trees, the consuming fire? Was John thinking, "Is this one whom I called 'mightier than I' really the Messiah?"

A wavering of faith is not unnatural. John was in prison—waiting for his execution. So it's natural that he wondered if his faith had been misplaced. But what a lesson for us. When John's faith faltered, he stretched out his hand to Jesus. There are times in our life when we have doubts—and that's okay. It's not a negative thing at all to carry our doubts to Jesus. So John asks the question: "Are you the one or should we look for another?"

What follows the question seems to be out of place. "Jesus had just then cured many people of diseases, plagues, and evil spirits, and had given sight to many who were blind." It's simply a statement, but it is inserted in the text following the asking of John's question and preceding Jesus' answer.

But it's not out of place. It's a one-line detail of current happenings that set the stage for Jesus' response. "Go and tell John what you have seen and heard: the blind receive their sight, the lame walk, the lepers are cleansed, the deaf hear, the dead are raised, the poor have good news brought to them. And blessed is anyone who takes no offense at me" (vv. 22-23). In Perry County, Mississippi, where I grew up, we would put it this way: "The proof is in the pudding."

LISTENING IS THE MARK OF CARING

Here is an obvious confirmation: *the most important ingredient in the pudding of caring is listening.* The Bible has a lot to say about listening. The word "listen" is used over 185 times. The word "hear" is used over 450 times. Other forms of the words "listen" and "hear" are used over 600 times. That's nearly 1,200 times in total! Perhaps this is an indication that listening is difficult.

Speaking is not so difficult. We have something to say on just about any subject, but listening is something else. The turn and use of words in a phrase I heard recently lodged it firmly in my mind. The person, talking about the importance of listening, said, "I am trying to listen louder." The proof of the pudding of caring is the ingredient of listening.

Caring and listening are matters of Christian concern because *the proof in the pudding of Christianity is the ingredient of love.* A Methodist preacher colleague, Rodney Wilmoth, tells of purchasing a new car that had the automatic lights-off feature. Now there are some wonderful things about that feature—there's something about being able to drive into the garage where it's dark, and just get out of the car in the light and walk to the back door while the car lights are still on, and then have them turn off automatically. But everything about that wonderful feature was not wonderful for Rodney. He told about having people in restaurants tap on the window and point to the lights on his car. People stopped their cars and backed up to let him know that he had not turned his lights off.

The climax of that concern about his lights came when he parked in the garage at the medical center. Because it was darker inside the garage, his car-lights came on as he drove into the garage. As he was walking away from his car, a pickup truck stopped. The driver got out and called, "Hey, Buddy, your lights are on." He turned and gave him his usual courteous reply, "Thank you. They will go off by themselves." Just as he was saying that, a woman drove by, stopped her car, and vigorously pointed to his lighted automobile. Because her windows were rolled up, Rodney had to pantomime, "They will go off. Thank you!" He proceeded to walk on, and she proceeded to drive right into the back of the pickup truck that had stopped.

Those automatic lights caused Rodney to realize how many caring people there were around him. On the same day the woman ran into the pickup truck trying to tell him his lights were on, a story appeared in the *Omaha World Herald*, and Rodney read it. A sixty-eight-year-old man died while lying on a bus stop bench. Residents and employees of that busy part of the city said they did not see the man stretched out on that bench on that subfreezing day. The editorial said that "maybe if someone had seen the man a few hours earlier he could have been saved." Sharing that, Rodney made this observation: "I cannot take five steps away from my automobile without any number of persons showing their concern by telling me my lights are on, and yet hundreds of people can pass a major intersection and not take note of a man freezing to death on a bench."

A friend suggested the reason for this. "Maybe it is easier to be concerned about lights than lives. One can risk getting involved when it comes to helping another person with car lights, but it is often a different matter when it comes to getting involved in broken lives."

This brings us to the big point of Jesus' word to John. *The proof in the pudding of who you are is the ingredient of your actions.* That's what Jesus was telling John. If you want to know who I am, look at what I do.

I told the following story about John Lennon of the Beatles on a radio/television program called *Perceptions.* In 1978 Lennon had ceased to even resemble himself. Wasted by dieting, fasting, and self-induced vomiting, he weighed only 130 pounds. Drugged all day on Thai-stick, magic mushrooms, or heroin, he slept much of the time and spent his waking hours in a kind of trance. In his biography *The Lives of John Lennon*, Albert Goldman wrote: "Lennon had simply refused to pay the price for staying alive, the toll levied in terms of involvement, responsibility, and effort" ([Chicago: Chicago Review Press, 1988], p. 605).

Might we learn from Lennon? We stay alive only by involvement, responsibility, and effort. A few months after I told this story on my radio program, my administrative assistant received a telephone call. It was from Mr. Elliot Mintz, the lawyer of the estate of John Lennon. He had just received a call from some person in New York who had heard my "perception" about John Lennon and was concerned that I had painted a rather ugly picture about him. He had also gotten a call from Associated Press asking if he would like to respond to what I had said about Lennon. Mary, my assistant, was concerned that I might be sued by the estate of John Lennon. What I had said about him I had quoted from a book, and I had given that source. But I didn't know what the law was, thus I was naturally concerned. When I told Lennon's lawyer the story, he understood. However, he went to great lengths to tell me how the writer of that book had been misinformed, how the book had never amounted to much, and how John Lennon in his closing months had become a different person. He even sent me a script of a long, expansive interview that someone had conducted with Lennon before he died.

This lawyer wanted to correct an image of John Lennon that was abroad in the world—an image that comes from the fact that we are what we do. The proof is in the pudding.

After getting that call from the estate of John Lennon, I began to ask myself the questions: "If someone ever wrote a book about me, what would they be able to say? What kind of picture would they present?" As I thought about that, I knew whatever they wrote would be determined by my involvements. What claims my energy? What claims my resources? To what am I giving my life? You see, it's what we spend our lives for that really matters. That's the proof of the pudding.

QUESTIONS FOR REFLECTION

How can you improve your listening and caring? If someone wrote a book about you, what would it say? What kind of picture do you present to those around you?

23

Our God Is Consistent but Not Predictable

1 KINGS 8:31-40; LAMENTATIONS 3:1-24; PSALM 68:11-20

Solomon, following the reign of David, was given the task of building the Temple. It took him seven years. Built of cedar and cypress and overlaid with pure gold, it was something to behold. It was a magnificent gem of architecture. When it was finished, Solomon assembled the elders of Israel, the heads of the tribes, and the leaders of the ancestral houses of Israel. All was ready for the dedication. Throngs of awe-smitten people, full of holy expectation, filled the Temple as the priests placed the Ark of the Covenant under the wingspread of cherubim. All were pleased, but the simmering question was, "Would God make God's presence known?"

The priests came out of the holy place, and the people's expectation was fulfilled as a cloud filled the house of the Lord, "so that the priests could not stand to minister because of the cloud; for the glory of the LORD filled the house of the LORD" (8:11). God's glory filled the Temple. God was present.

In that setting of spellbinding mystery and awe, "Solomon [stands] before the altar of the LORD in the presence of all the assembly of Israel" and prays. He begins the prayer by acknowledging God's transcendence and immanence all in one breath. "There is no God like you in heaven above [God is transcendent] . . . keeping covenant and steadfast love for your servants who walk before you with all their heart [God is immanent]" (vv. 22-23).

We now have the full revelation of God in Jesus Christ and need not be confused about God's nature and ask as did Solomon, "Will God indeed dwell on the earth?" (1 Kings 8:27). Yet we continue to ask the question. We see the starving masses in the Sudan, the killings in Israel and Palestine, the ravaging wars in Iraq and Afghanistan, the rising number of homeless people in the United States, and the wildfire pandemic of HIV/AIDS and we ask from deep within our soul, "Will God dwell upon the earth? Will God make God's presence known to us?"

GOD'S STEADFAST LOVE

At the heart of Solomon's prayer is the plea for forgiveness. The Bible is the one book that teaches that God completely forgives sin. There is consistency with Solomon in the praying of God's people.

Fast-forward to 586 B.C. The holy city of Jerusalem was attacked, conquered, and destroyed by the Babylonians. The Temple of Solomon was leveled. The best of Israel's citizens were exiled to Babylon. Soon thereafter some anonymous court official in Jerusalem, a man of deep faith, wrote Lamentations, a vivid and emotional expression of the horror of this event, a profound expression of national distress. Right in the middle of the woe and heartbreak is an exquisite statement of thanksgiving (Lam. 3). Not even the blackness of national disaster could blind this man to the constant goodness of God. And on that goodness he based his hopes for the future.

In the dedication of the temple, Solomon had prayed for forgiveness, believing that God would keep his covenant and steadfast love. Now, in the presence of the destruction of the temple in which Solomon's prayer had been offered, in the setting of devastation, the Lord's faithfulness is remembered. The nature of God is remembered as the writer names God's "steadfast love" (3:22, 32), "mercies" (v. 22), and "compassion" (v. 32).

Though surrounded by deep darkness, unexplainable evil, and suffering that has no known cause, the glory and goodness of God is celebrated.

> The steadfast love of the LORD never ceases,
>   his mercies never come to an end;
> they are new every morning;
>   great is your faithfulness. (3:22-23)

This is not only the witness of Solomon and the unknown writer of Lamentations; it the glorious witness of both the Old and New Testaments. Reflect and rejoice in that witness.

NEVER-ENDING MERCIES

God's love is consistent. Verse 22 says it clearly and beautifully: "The steadfast love of the LORD never ceases, / his mercies never come to an end." God is more dependable than the tides, more consistent than the sunrise.

God may be consistent, but he is not always predictable. God is full of gracious surprises. His mercies "are new every morning." The psalmist prayed,

> Blessed be the Lord,
> who *daily* bears us up. (68:19, emphasis added)

God told Isaiah: "I am about to create new heavens and a new earth" 65:17). Jesus talked about new wine requiring new wineskins. He gave us a new commandment and a new covenant in his blood. Finally, in the revelation of John, he declared: "Behold, I make all things new" (Rev. 21:5 KJV).

The Grace-Filled Life

God's love is consistent, yes, but always full of newness. Because God is faithful, his love consistent and full of surprises, *we are never without hope.*

> "The LORD is my portion," says my soul,
> "therefore I will hope in him." (Lam. 3:24)

Who would have dreamed that the Soviet Union would close up its communistic shop and open wide to the outside world? Who would have ever dreamed that Communist Red Army trucks that once brought fear to the hearts of Soviet Christians would one day be leased by the Bible League to transport Bibles across that land?

God is faithful. God is consistent in his love, and is always surprising us. Here is a demonstration of those characteristics of God in a person. The faculty and trustees of Asbury Seminary voted to confer on Boris Trajkovski the honorary Doctor of Humane Letters degree. Boris was the President of Macedonia. He was not able to come to our country to receive it, so our plan was to confer the degree in his capital city, Skopje. We were shocked and saddened early on February 27, 2004, to learn of his death in a plane crash.

Boris was a friend. Jerry (my wife) and I met him in 1988. As Chair of World Evangelism of the World Methodist Council, I was in Macedonia encouraging the Methodist churches that had been courageously hanging on in spite of severe oppression and persecution. Boris was a young attorney, a devoted and practicing Christian. It didn't surprise us later, when he was elected president of his country, that he played the major role in his government's relationship to the huge number of ethnic Albanians, and that he helped save Macedonia from being another Bosnia or Kosovo.

Time and again, when we were with him privately or when he spoke publicly, he emphasized that there is no true peace apart from the peace found in Jesus Christ. He made this surprising observation as the president of a nation that was war-torn. "There will never be peace if we believe we are able to achieve that peace with our own hands. All we will ever be able to achieve is manage conflict, not bring true peace. It is beyond us as human beings . . . sinful human beings . . . to achieve true peace, because that can be found only in Jesus Christ."

In his presence, as well as in his words, you could never doubt the source of his hope. As the presence of the Living Lord had empowered him in his difficult work as President of Macedonia, I'm sure the Lord was present with him in death. He was on his way to Ireland to continue negotiation for Macedonia to enter the European Union, when his plane went down. He ended up in a more glorious union: around the throne, in the presence of God, praising and worshiping the one whose steadfast love never ceases, and whose mercies never come to an end.

QUESTIONS FOR REFLECTION

Recall an experience that confirms God's mercies never coming to an end. In what way may you be stuck in the past? With whom do you need to share in a way that will give them hope of God's steadfast love?

24

STAND ON YOUR FEET AND I WILL SPEAK TO YOU

EZEKIEL 2:1-7; PROVERBS 4:10-19

John Birkbeck, a Scottish Presbyterian preacher, is a person around whom for me a whole cluster of memories is gathered. During my tenure as the World Editor of *The Upper Room*, he was the editor of the British edition of *The Upper Room*.

John introduced me to the Scottish preacher Robert Murray McCheyne. I hope I will never forget what John brought to my attention in one of Mc-Cheyne's books. "The greatest need of my congregation is my own personal holiness." I also found this true in my years of pastoral ministry. I believe it has meaning not only for pastors but for all of God's people.

GOD SPEAKS. DO YOU LISTEN?

A couple of years ago I was smitten in my heart by a word I heard in the ordination service of the Free Methodist Church.

> The people to whom I am sending you are obstinate and stubborn. Say to them, "This is what the sovereign LORD says." And whether they listen or fail to listen—for they are a rebellious house—they will know that a prophet has been among them. (Ezek. 2:4-5 NIV)

In Ezekiel 2, Ezekiel is sharing his personal story of God coming to him in a vision and calling him to be a prophet/priest. He sees the "glory of Yahweh" coming down from heaven, and it is so overwhelming that he falls on his face. But the Lord will not let him remain there: "Son of man, stand up on your feet, and I will speak to you." And the Lord does speak. The message Ezekiel is to preach is given to him in a kind of scroll. So Ezekiel receives his appointment. It is not a promising situation. Not the planting of a new church that is sure to grow in an exciting fashion. Not to be the senior pastor of First Church downtown, which has tremendous influence in the entire community. Not an appointment to a rapidly growing church in suburbia. It is a hard call, and God makes it clear. In exercising his prophetic office, Ezekiel will have to preach to deaf ears and dwell among scorpions.

A HUMBLE WILLINGNESS TO RECEIVE

In this call of Ezekiel, there are some lessons, and some powerful promises not only to Ezekiel but to all God's people. First, God says, "Stand up on your feet and I will speak to you" (2:1). The lesson? We are to listen. Our stance must always be a receptive one. "Speak, Lord, your servant is listening."

Two, after hearing God tell him to "stand on his feet" so that he might speak to him, Ezekiel says, "As he spoke, the Spirit came into me and raised me to my feet, and I heard him speaking to me." The lesson? *It is not our ability to do what God calls us to do but our willingness to respond, attempt what he calls us to, that releases God's power.* God called Ezekiel, "Stand up on your feet," but then—as Ezekiel says—"a Spirit came to me and set me on my feet."

We may express this second lesson in this fashion: God does not call us to a ministry or a mission that we can accomplish in our own strength and with our own resources—but only with his divine aid. In that way, we're kept on our knees, dependent upon him.

Then there is a third lesson and a promise. Look at Ezekiel 3:1-3:

> And he said to me, "Son of man, eat what is before you, eat this scroll; then go and speak to the house of Israel." . . . So I ate it, and it tasted as sweet as honey in my mouth. (NIV)

The lesson? *We must become one with God's word.* What we say must be matched by how we live. That's what holiness is all about.

GOD'S CALL TO HOLINESS

God's call is unmistakable: "Be holy as I am holy." There should be about Christ followers that which is distinctive: the way we relate to each other, the way we think about and respond to the poor, how we spend our money, how we care for God's creation. The book of Proverbs makes the case for the distinct character of God's people. Proverbs is in large part practical wisdom about character and holiness. We see this in the "parental advice" of Proverbs 4. The contrast between righteousness and wickedness is vividly stated. "The path of the righteous is like the light of dawn, / which shines brighter and brighter until full day. / The way of the wicked is like deep darkness; / they do not know what they stumble over" (4:18-19).

The distinctiveness of our character—the way we live, our "holiness"—is our most powerful witness. God makes this clear as he instructs Ezekiel:

> I will show the holiness of my great name. . . . Then the nations will know that I am the LORD . . . when I show myself holy through you before their eyes. (36:23 NIV)

Therefore, it is through you, my people, God says, that who I am will be demonstrated.

QUESTIONS FOR REFLECTION

How does your life witness to your faith? What does God's call, "Be holy as I am holy," mean to you?

25

THE PLEA OF GRACE

LEVITICUS 4:1-12; LUKE 13:1-9

The oil well of a man in East Liverpool, Ohio, caught on fire. It was uncontrollable, and there were no fire stations anywhere near. The man offered a $3,000 reward to whoever could put it out. All the fire companies from the surrounding cities and villages came and tried, but the fire was so intense no one could get near enough to even attempt putting it out. Then the volunteer fire brigade from Calcutta, a tiny nearby town arrived on the scene. They had an old fire truck, one ladder, three buckets of sand, a small tank of water, and one blanket. They came wheeling into the oil field and, to everyone's surprise, they didn't stop at some distance from the raging fire, but boldly and bravely, risking the "fire of hell," they rolled right up to the blaze. They jumped out, climbed the ladder, poured the tank of water and the buckets of sand on the fire, threw their blanket over the now diminished blaze and completely smothered it. The $3,000 was theirs.

"What are you going to do with this money," the relieved oil well owner asked. The brigade leader responded, "First of all, we're going to put new brakes on our truck."

APPEARANCES SOMETIMES DECEIVE

Luke 13 introduces the story of the barren fig tree and makes the point that things are not always what they seem. This is clearly a parable of judgment, but it is also a parable of grace. The parable is introduced by a question about sin and its consequences. Jesus is clear in his teaching: *all affliction and suffering are not due to sin or wrongdoing, but all sin and wrongdoing bring affliction and suffering.*

"Unless you repent, you will all perish" is the dominant note of the parable, but it is helpful to remember the context. The occasion was recalled when some Galileans were offering sacrifices to God—perhaps protesting the oppressive rule of Rome. While they were engaged in worship, Roman soldiers slaughtered them mercilessly. The blood of the worshipers and that of the animal sacrifices were mingled on the altar.

Before Jesus tells the parable, he is asked, "Do you think that because these Galileans suffered in this way they were worse sinners than all other Galileans?" The belief of these questioners was that where there is great suffering there is, of necessity, great sin, because suffering was punishment for sin. Jesus responded

The Grace-Filled Life

with a resounding NO, and added that sobering word: "but unless you repent, you will all perish as they did."

Jesus is not denying the fact that sin and wrongdoing have tangible consequences, but he is clarifying an important truth. Calamity is not necessarily the result of sin. The rains fall on the just as well as the unjust. The best among us do not escape misfortune and suffering. Having clarified that, Jesus tells his parable to underscore the fact that judgment is certain.

George Buttrick, one of the most outstanding preachers of the twentieth century, reminds us that this parable could be referring to the Jewish nation and her faith. Israel

> had prospered on a sunny hillside of God's favor, not in worldly bounty or in political dominion, but in the richer blessing of prophetic guidance. What other nation had been blessed by so noble a succession of lighted souls? Abraham, Moses, David, Isaiah, Jeremiah, Amos, Hosea, John the Baptist . . . and Jesus! No land, great or small, in ancient or modern times, can match that galaxy of inspired leadership. Their insight is still the chart and compass of our voyaging world. But this intensive privilege (of Israel) had produced no good character. (*The Parables of Jesus* [New York: Harper and Brothers Publishers, 1928], p. 108)

What lessons are here for us? Is there a nation more blessed than we? The natural blessings God has bestowed upon us are beyond number. Yet we continue to ravage our environment in destructive ways. No less than 30 million people are living in poverty. The unemployment rate is nearing 10 percent. We have a drug culture that could lead to our demise. Racism still eats at the soul of our country. We are presently fighting wars in Afghanistan and Iraq, and another is threatened in Iran. The sword of Damocles hangs over our head in the form of a raging national neurotic insecurity. We have to ask, how long is the Lord going to abide our sinfulness, our cynical, self-serving pride?

Back to Israel, to whom the parable of the barren fig tree might have referred. Moses and Aaron, having led them through the wilderness, after their freedom from captivity in Egypt, are charged with helping the Israelites establish their calling and character as God's people. God had his unique claim on Israel, "You shall be for me a priestly kingdom and a holy nation" (Exod. 19:6). The book of Leviticus is a manual for the sacrificial system and a guide to the offerings and for ethical behavior. Its purpose was

> to awaken people to sin as God sees it, and according to the covenant relationship between the Lord and their tribes. Moses is to teach them how to follow the paths of righteousness in formal patterns of worship and how to make sacrifices . . . to cover their iniquities. (*Wesley Study Bible*, Introduction to Leviticus, p. 121)

Sin had to be dealt with—even unintentional sin (Lev. 4). The "law" pre-scribed a prescription of acknowledgment, repentance, and sacrifice. Unless sin was dealt with in this fashion it would be destructive to the individual and the nation. So there is a connection not only between the parable of the bar-ren fig tree and Israel but also between any nation and any person. Register the lessons.

One, *unfruitfulness is not allowed in God's vineyard.* Flannery O'Connor asks a probing question, "Have you ever looked inside yourself and seen what you are not?" What we are not, but should be, is what will bring judgment upon us. Two, fruitfulness in God's vineyard means at least this: *because of you, the milk of human kindness is available to someone;* because of you, the Spirit of Christ is daily set loose in the world.

My friend Sir Alan Walker tells of the Australian poet Victor Daley being tenderly cared for in a Catholic hospital as he was dying. One of his last acts was to thank the nuns for all their kindness to him. "Don't thank us," their leader said, "thank the grace of God." Very perceptively, the poet asked, "But aren't you the grace of God?"

The grace of God is not magical; it doesn't work automatically. It works practically, and you can trace the course of grace through our lives.

THE PRACTICAL WORK OF GRACE

The third lesson in this parable is that *the worthless fig tree had its intercessor.* The judgment "cut it down!" was met with the plea of the vineyard keeper, "Let it alone for one more year, until I dig around it and put manure on it. If it bears fruit next year, well and good; but if not, you can cut it down" (Luke 13:8-9).

More than a hint of God's grace is here. To be sure, there is a law of use-lessness that induces death; but there is another law, maybe a deeper law in God's kingdom economy: the law of pitying grace. Abraham nobly interceded for Sodom; Moses offered his own life with strong tears and utter devotion for an idolatrous people. And Jesus! Imagine it. While he was speaking that stern word of warning and judgment, he was getting ready to go to the Cross; and by his righteous death, to act as the great high priest, of whom the priests of Leviti-cus were a dim foretelling, who pleads the cause of all sinners.

"Unless you repent," Jesus said, "you will likewise perish." That is the re-sounding note of judgment. But the plea comes, "Give it another year"—the plea of grace. Because Christ is all grace, grace will be his response if . . . if we repent and seek that second chance.

QUESTIONS FOR REFLECTION

What is going on in our nation that may be signs of our betraying God's blessings? What weaknesses, mistakes, and sins do you need to confess and for which you need to repent? Are you walking with God or away from God?

26

WORKING OUT OUR SALVATION

LUKE 15:1-7; PHILIPPIANS 2:12-13

I will never forget my first visit to China. President Nixon had visited the previous year and the "bamboo curtain" was just beginning to open a bit. The Christian church had been outlawed by Chairman Mao and his revolution. Though they were "underground," we knew there were Christians, but it was not easy to communicate with them.

I was with a small group headed by Harry Haines, the Director of the Methodist Committee on Overseas Relief. We were there not as Christian leaders but as tourists. Our purpose, however, was to make contact with Christians as we could without putting their lives in danger, and to discover how we might move forward in relationship and support. Our meetings were secretive. It was risky for Chinese Christians to meet openly with foreigners.

One late night, we met with four couples. All had suffered from the revolution. Two of the men had been separated from their wives for fifteen years, sent away to work as peasants and be "re-educated." The other two men had been professors in the university but were forced to labor in factories, as were all four women.

We knew we were under surveillance; every move we made while there was observed. Yet as we gathered with those courageous Christians, they wanted to read Scripture, pray, and sing. We sang quietly, almost in a whisper, their two favorites: "What a Friend We Have in Jesus" and "Amazing Grace."

GOD WILL FIND US

The fifteenth chapter of Luke's Gospel has been called "the gospel within the gospel." Here we have Jesus' parables of "the lost sheep," "the lost coin," and the "prodigal son" (which is really the story of two "lost sons").

These parables make clear the heart of Christianity, that we don't find our way to God, God finds his way to us. Amazing grace has nothing to do with our finding God. "I once was *lost*, but *now* I'm found." Judaism and Christianity are the world religions that share this message. In every other religion we have to go to God. The job of priests in these other religions is to mediate between people and God, to appease God through sacrifices so God will accept us. Not so with Christianity. The three parables of Jesus proclaim beautifully and clearly that God seeks and finds us. God never gives up on anyone.

It is not because we have repented that God comes to us. When we accept the fact that God comes to us, we find the grace that brings the genuine repentance that changes our life. But salvation is more than coming home. Grace enables us to repent and return to the Father's embrace of love, but grace also enables us to do as Paul called us to do: to "work out your own salvation with fear and trembling" (Phil. 2:12).

How are we to receive this word when we are so immersed in Paul's radical understanding of salvation by grace through faith, "not of works, lest any man should boast" (Eph. 2:9 KJV)? Paul follows his word about working out our salvation with the claim, "For it is God who is at work in you, enabling you both to will and to work for his good pleasure." John Wesley reminds us that here is a clear expression of the interaction of divine grace with human will and action. "First, God works; therefore you can work. Secondly, God works; therefore you must work" (*Wesley Study Bible*, note to 2:12-13, pp. 1441-42).

It is all grace, but we participate. We allow the mind of Christ to be in us. By will and discipline, we cultivate the mind of Christ in us. We are to work out our salvation—to grow in maturity, to grow up into the full measure of the stature of Christ.

OBEDIENCE AND ABANDONMENT

Paul does not mean for this section of Scripture to be his only discussion of how we are to work out our salvation. However, there are some signal clues for us, some things around which we can build and order our life as we seek to work out our salvation in fear and trembling. The clues are in two words: obedience and abandonment.

The first is a call to *obedience*. The central message of the New Testament is that we are saved by grace through faith. Grace is unmerited, undeserved, unlimited, given freely by God. The ultimate expression of grace is in the death of his son, Jesus, as satisfaction for our sins. What God, in and through Christ, has done for us can be appropriated by anyone only by faith. But faith is not simply believing with the mind; it involves our wills and our emotions. The best word for it is *trust*.

Faith is not just a passive, grateful reception of God's mercy; rather, it is an active entrustment of ourselves to that mercy in the hands of God. Trust is the best understanding of faith, because trust is both a verb and a noun. *We have trust*; we also can *trust someone*. Faith is a noun but does not have a verb form. We can't say, "I faith you." We can say, "I trust you." We are justified then not just by believing but by entrusting ourselves to him.

This is the first signal clue for our working out our salvation with fear and trembling—obedience. See it in a person.

Dag Hammarskjöld, the first UN Secretary General, was a rare example of a modern Christian mystic who was also a man of the world. While living his busy, productive life, he bore an eloquent witness and a challenging word to the meaning of obedience. He said on one occasion:

> I don't know who or what put the question, I don't even know when it was put, I don't even remember answering, but at some moment I did answer yes, to someone. And from that hour, I was certain that life was meaningful for me, and that therefore my life, in self-surrender, has a goal. (*Markings* [New York: Alfred A. Knopf, 1964], p. 180)

The statement not only witnesses to obedience but to servanthood. The Who, who always puts the question, is God.

The second word that provides a signal clue for working out our salvation is even more radical: *abandonment*. Obedience is essential, but for Paul there was a degree of obedience that deserves special note: abandonment. We see it in Paul himself. The extravagance of his obedience is shocking. "I am being poured out like a drink offering on the sacrifice and service coming from your faith" (Phil. 2:17 NIV).

It may be that you join me in confessing that my biggest problem—not only as it relates to how I express my obedience to Christ but in my basic approach to life—is an unwillingness to give up control. To abandon myself in faith to Christ is hard even to talk about, much less to do. Only in trusting Christ can we come to a point of abandonment, a willingness to put our lives into the Lord's hands, believing we don't need to, nor can we, control the future. The future belongs to God.

Words like obedience and discipline and abandonment fall heavy on our ears unless we keep the ears of our hearts tuned to Christ. A few years ago, I did a filmed conversation with the Russian Orthodox Archbishop Anthony Bloom, who has written so helpfully about a life of prayer. When I questioned him about ordinary persons living the contemplative life of prayer in the everyday world, he used an image of joyful obedience and abandonment he had gotten from Evelyn Underhill. He said a Christian should be like a sheepdog. When the shepherd wants the dog to do something, the dog lies down at the shepherd's feet, looks intently into the shepherd's eyes, and listens without budging until he has understood clearly the mind of his master. Then he jumps to his feet, he runs out to do it, and at no moment does he cease wagging his tail.

Working out our salvation is the ultimate joy of life.

QUESTIONS FOR REFLECTION

How is the call to obedience working in your life? To what degree is abandonment to God's will operative in your life? Is there someone who needs your help in finding God in a deeper, more significant way?

27

STANDING IN THE BREACH

EZEKIEL 21:1-17; 22:17-31

In September of 1997 there was a groundbreaking service for a Catholic cathedral that was going to be constructed in Los Angeles. The Diocese of Los Angeles commissioned the famous Spanish architect José Rafael Moneo to design the building. There were models of the cathedral at the groundbreaking service, and on the basis of the models, a Los Angeles Times reporter wrote a review of the cathedral. This is a part of what the reporter said, "Moneo is creating an alternate world to the everyday world that surrounds the cathedral, a testimony to grandeur of the human spirit, an antidote to a world that is increasingly spiritually empty."

Then he wrote this sentence, "The cathedral, set in the midst of the secular city, will be an enclave of resistance." What an image—the church an enclave of resistance. My friend Mark Trotter, who shared that story, suggested that that phrase should be a part of the mission statement of every church in the city, "an enclave of resistance against all that diminishes human life" ("An Enclave of Resistance," a sermon preached by Mark Trotter, First United Methodist Church, San Diego, California, October 5, 1997).

Whether it should be a part of the mission statement of every church or not is not my concern—but that it should be a factor in our awareness of who we are as the church is absolutely crucial. There is a sense in which that is what Israel was called to be in the culture in which she was set—an enclave of resistance. God chose Israel to be "a holy nation, God's own people" (1 Pet. 2:9). The church, as the "new Israel," was to function in the same fashion.

Along with all the prophets, Ezekiel constantly confronted his people about their failure to be holy and righteous, to sustain their integrity as the "people of God." His time setting was five hundred and fifty years before the birth of Jesus. The entire Middle Eastern world was ruled by Babylon. The tiny kingdom of Judah fell when King Jehoiachin surrendered to the Babylonian armies of Nebuchadnezzar in 589 B.C. All her artists, her merchants, her prophets were systematically removed from their beloved country and resettled along the Euphrates River. The chosen people were in exile.

Ezekiel, a young priest, was among those deported from Jerusalem to Babylon. He witnessed the life of his exiled people and, in a vision, saw his nation finally destroyed, even, to his horror, the holy city and the Temple. The theme of individual and corporate responsibility to fulfill the covenant requirements and the inevitable results of refusing to do so run throughout Ezekiel's prophecy.

The Grace-Filled Life

God's people were called to be holy as God is holy. In the first verses of chapter 22, Ezekiel enumerates the sins of Israel and the list includes the violation of all ten, core commandments, along with other priestly concerns about holy living. Our particular reading from Ezekiel 22 is a dramatic expression of how Israel and her leaders had failed. They have "smeared whitewash on their false vision and lies . . . profaned holy things . . . made no distinction between the holy and the common . . . the unclean and the clean . . . oppressed the poor and needy, extorted from the alien."

He concludes, "and I sought for anyone among them who would repair the wall and stand in the breach before me on behalf of the land, so that I would not destroy it; but I found no one" (22:30).

Old Testament scholar Gerhard von Rad says that more than any other prophet, Ezekiel is influenced by the priestly religious life of Israel, and indeed his prophetic ministry is a priestly one. He says that Ezekiel is the first prophet consciously to enter this new sphere of activity, which may be described as "sure of souls" (The Message of the Prophets [New York: Harper & Row, 1972], p. 200). His calling was not just the traditional prophetic task of addressing the community and the nation—speaking the word of God to them—but also caring for individuals, assisting persons in realizing their own situation in the eyes of God.

The role of a prophet/priest is to speak to the people for God, and to speak to God for the people.

The prophet/priest must speak to the people for God, reminding them that holiness is not an option for God's people. It is not likely that our prophetic words will be heard unless and until there is at least a remnant of faithful people who seek to be, as Paul says, "imitators of God, as beloved children, and live in love, as Christ loved us and gave himself up for us, a fragrant offering and sacrifice to God" (Eph 5:1-2).

What a powerful reminder. Our prophetic/priestly function of speaking to the people for God requires identification with our people, a passion for their salvation, and a compassion that calls for a willingness to suffer, even to die for their sake. Ezekiel used the image of a watchman. In his day, the Jews had the custom of building watchtowers in their fields and vineyards for a person to keep watch at harvest time to warn of approaching hostile people coming to steal the harvest. Ezekiel was keenly aware that God had called him to be a watchman, a messenger to warn the Israelites of the impending destruction awaiting those who did not give up their evil ways. Is it too much of a stretch for us to think of the church as "an enclave of resistance," speaking and living in such a way as to warn people of the consequences of sin and the danger of living wickedly?

Our debauched culture underscores the need for holiness, for "an enclave of resistance" that keeps sounding God's call, "Be holy as I am holy."

But not only does the prophet/priest speak to the people for God, he speaks to God for the people. Early in his book, Ezekiel makes it clear that not only is he, as a watchman, to be faithful in warning the people but also that if he failed to do so, he would be held responsible.

As Yahweh made Ezekiel responsible, has he not made us responsible for the souls committed to our care in the ministries to which we are called? It was rather dramatic with Ezekiel. If he allowed the wicked to die unwarned, Yahweh threatened to require their lives at the prophet's own hands. So Yahweh says to him, "Therefore groan, son of man! Groan before them with broken heart and bitter grief" (21:6 NIV). Here is the dynamic of speaking to the people for God and speaking to God for the people: groaning. It is both a prophetic and a priestly action, both intervention and intercession.

Who are the people in our community who have yet to receive a clear message from you personally, and from the church, that you deeply care for them and that God loves them?

What about the poor? Are we speaking to our people for God who, if he loves one people more than any other, it is the poor? What about the working poor—chief among them single mothers?

What of the vast segment of people in every community—especially in our cities—for whom Christ and his church are strangers? Are we ordering our life and worship, our ministry and mission in a way that speaks a language they understand and offers what will meet their needs where they are, not where you would like for them to be?

What about the recovering people—those seeking freedom from drugs and alcohol? Is our church a community of welcome and hospitality that will help them break the chains of shame and blame?

"Son of man, groan!" God said to Ezekiel, and says to us. Show the people that you care, that you speak for a God who loves us, who forgives our iniquities and heals our diseases, who restores us to wholeness and gives us joy, and to whom we are making intercession on their behalf.

QUESTIONS FOR REFLECTION

What is the word from God that our nation most needs to hear? That your community needs to hear? That your church needs to hear? Who are the people in your community to whom you need to speak God's word and for whom you need to speak to God?

28

WATERING THE GARDEN OF OUR LIFE

PROVERBS 11:24-25; COLOSSIANS 1:21-23; LUKE 19:11-27

Across Northern Africa stretches the largest desert in the world, the Sahara. Mile after mile of scorching, shifting sand stretches from east to west, farther than the distance from New York to San Francisco. The Sahara is almost as large as the United States.

Temperatures can reach 130 degrees Fahrenheit, making breathing almost impossible. Yet at the eastern edge of this earth-oven is the Nile Valley, one of the richest, most fertile valleys in the world. The Nile River, the longest river in the world, flows through the valley. Before the building of the Aswan Dam, this great river overflowed every year, bringing rich tropical soil from the jungles of Central Africa and depositing layer after layer of this rich soil all over the valley. What the Nile did, until it was contained, is a picture that is repeated over and over again in Proverbs. It is explicitly stated in Proverbs 11:25: "A generous person will be enriched, / and one who gives water will get water." Like the Nile, the mere flow of our life is meaningless in this desert world of today. It is only when our heart overflows generously that we are enriched to the point of life being meaningful. It is when our heart overflows generously that we provide refreshing water for all the parched lives around us.

REFRESHED BY A GENEROUS HEART

Read again our selected verses from Proverbs 11. Does it remind you of how Jesus said we are to give? "Give, and it will be given to you. A good measure, pressed down, shaken together, running over, will be put into your lap; for the measure you give will be the measure you get back" (Luke 6:38).

Does it remind you of Jesus' parable of the ten pounds in Luke 19? Recall how he closed his teaching with that parable: "I tell you, to all those who have, more will be given; but from those who have nothing, even what they have will be taken away" (v. 26).

Does the Proverb teaching remind you of how Paul described Jesus' giving of himself to us in Colossians?

At one time you all had your backs turned to God, thinking rebellious thoughts of him, giving him trouble every chance you got. But now, by giving himself completely at the Cross, actually *dying* for you, Christ brought you over to God's side and put your lives together, whole and holy in his presence. You don't walk away from a gift like that! (Col. 1:20-21 *THE MESSAGE*)

We are not to glory in our past sins, but we must also not forget them. As growing Christians, we must never assume we have always been what we now are. What we are as Christians is all by the grace of God. To be preoccupied with sin is unhealthy spiritually and emotionally—even relationally. Yet to forget who we are and who we have been is the doorway to spiritual pride and a roadblock to spiritual growth.

Genuine self-awareness—remembering who we are and where we have been—fills us with gratitude, and gratitude *always* expresses itself in generosity. That's the way we keep the garden of our life watered.

Someone once designated three great killers in modern life: the telephone, the clock, and the calendar. Perhaps today we might add: the cell phone, the PDA, and the Internet. They are the symbols of hurried, hectic living. The tyranny of the phone is interruption, not only through a busy day but often into the night. The tyranny of the clock has to do with appointments, all the things we have to do and the pressure to get them done on time. The tyranny of the calendar is apprehension about the future. We're often rendered impotent by our fear of the future. Our gadgets may be newer, but the tyrannies remain.

GIVING FREELY, GROWING RICHER

I believe we have overlooked one of the greatest medicines for our healing and wholeness. It is the medicine of liberality—being willing to give. Because we're locked up in ourselves, the chief malady of our time is that we are selfish. We're fearful—fearful in relationships, fearful about material security, fearful about our future, fearful about the future of our children, fearful about the political and economic plight of our nation, fearful about the rampage of deadly diseases such as cancer over which we have no control, fearful about the threat of AIDS and "swine flu."

We try to protect ourselves, look out for our own selves and our own security, so we lock ourselves in and hide. But rather than leave ourselves high and dry, we need to appropriate the wisdom of Proverbs, which calls us to tend to our garden and let the water of generosity flow—to become giving folks, "giving freely, yet growing richer."

There is a wonderful story about Maya Angelou. When she become an agnostic, she said that it wasn't that she stopped believing in God, just that God no longer frequented the neighborhoods that she frequented. She was taking voice lessons at the time and her teacher gave her an exercise where she was to read out of a religious pamphlet. The reading ended with these words: "God loves me." She finished the reading and put the pamphlet down. The teacher said, "I want you to read that last sentence again." So she picked it up, read it again, this time somewhat sarcastically, then put it down again. The teacher said, "Read it again." She read it again. Then she described what happened.

> After about the seventh repetition I began to sense there might be some truth in this statement. That there was a possibility that God really loves me, Maya Angelou. I suddenly began to cry at the grandness of it all. I knew if God loved me, I could do wonderful things. I could do great things. I could learn anything. I could achieve anything. For what could stand against me with God, since one person, any person, with God forms a majority now? (Mark Trotter, *Collected Sermons* [Christian Globe Networks, 2007])

When we learn that, the next step is to respond in gratitude. We learn that values in life are not measured by material things. Consider how we think about political or social issues like health care, minimum wage, and public education. Consider the current ongoing debate about "torture." It is easy to misplace values, not only in relation to material things, but in the whole of life. A good measure is to continually examine our attitudes and actions by asking: *To what degree am I putting myself in the center of things, rather than putting others and Kingdom values first?*

One of my two brothers was killed years ago in an industrial accident. He was killed because of nothing but the carelessness of a workman. I overcame the bitterness of that experience and the anger and the hate that was cultivated in my life as a result of such a waste of life only by the fact that I knew that my brother died seeking to save three other men who were caught in the dilemma caused by that workman who had left a gas valve open in the hull of the ship. I knew he lost his life by giving it for someone else.

To keep life for ourselves is to lose it. To lay our lives down in full-scale devotion for others is to find it. That's the way to water the garden of our lives. "Giving freely, yet growing richer." The power for that is our relationship with Jesus. "But now, by giving himself completely at the Cross, actually *dying* for you, Christ brought you over to God's side and put your lives together, whole and holy in his presence. You don't walk away from a gift like that!" (Col. 1:20-21 *THE MESSAGE*)

QUESTIONS FOR REFLECTION

How generous are you with your time? your money? your talent? What is holding you back from being more generous? What makes your heart overflow with joy?

29

SUBMISSION IS NOT A DIRTY WORD

PROVERBS 12:1-7; COLOSSIANS 3:12-25

When our oldest daughter, Kim, and I first began working on her wedding ceremony, she had the idea that she wanted to make a contribution to it, and she did—in a beautiful and meaningful way, writing some of the liturgy and planning the entire service of worship. But when it came to the vows, she thought she might make them more modern and up-to-date. It didn't take her long to discover that she couldn't improve on what is there.

Do you remember those questions? Will you have this woman to be your wedded wife, to live together in the holy estate of matrimony? Will you love her, Comfort her, honor and keep her in sickness and in health, and forsaking all others keep you only unto her as long as you both shall live? More mysterious than those particular questions are the specific vows the church invites the couple to make to each other. I, John, take thee, Kim, to be my wedded wife, to have and to hold from this day forward, for better or worse, for richer or poorer, in sickness and in health, to love and to cherish, as long as life shall last. In the mystery and the absurdity of those questions and those vows lies the uniqueness of Christian marriage.

In his Letter to the Colossians, Paul offers a challenging word,

> Wives, be subject to your husbands, as is fitting in the Lord. Husbands, love your wives, and do not be harsh with them. Children, obey your parents in everything, for this pleases the Lord. Fathers, do not provoke your children, lest they become discouraged. (3:18-21 RSV)

It is easy to miss the core meaning of this passage. The key is the conditional phrase at the close of verse 18, "*as is fitting in the Lord.*" Paul centers his teaching about home—about marriage and family—in Christ. Unless you begin there, nothing Paul says makes sense.

Before Paul, Jesus' attitude toward women and marriage was revolutionary. He saw and treated women as persons of worth, not as playthings for sexual gratification or household maids or merely agents of procreation. On one occasion, the Pharisees sought to entangle him in a dispute about divorce. He refused to simply address their specific question. In his compassion and commitment to women, he forced them to look at the original and eternal intention for marriage (see Mark 10:2-11),

But from the beginning of creation, "God made them male and female." For this reason a man shall leave his father and mother and be joined to his wife, and the two shall become one flesh. . . . Therefore what God has joined together, let no one separate. (Mark 10:6-9)

Paul followed Jesus. He talked about relationships "as fitting in the Lord" (Col. 3:18). *Commitment to each other is grounded in and finds its source in our faith in Christ.*

In his Letter to the Ephesians (chapters 5 and 6), where he deals with this same issue, Paul says to men: "Husbands, love your wives, as Christ loved the church and gave himself up for her" (5:25). He founded his teaching on the fact that a person in Christ has a new center of reference, a new Lord of life, and thus operates out of a totally new understanding of reality. People are brothers and sisters, all recipients of grace; and in the eyes of the Lord there is no distinction in worth between male and female. We miss a huge part of the meaning of his teaching if we focus too narrowly on his word, "Wives, be subject to your husbands as you are to the Lord" (5:22).

OUT OF REVERENCE FOR CHRIST

Submission is a dirty word in the vocabulary of many. We don't like the notion of submission, no matter how it comes to us, and when it comes in this way—standing alone—it's repulsive and we naturally are repelled. We need to remember that *submission* was considered one of the distinctive markings of a Christian lifestyle. "Be subject to one another out of reverence for Christ" are the words Paul used for his teaching about marriage and family with the Ephesians (5:21). He follows that admonition for all Christians with two verses that must be held together: Verse 22: "Wives, be subject to your husbands as you are to the Lord." And verse 25: "Husbands, love your wives, just as Christ loved the church and gave himself up for her." Those two verses, which specifically instruct the relationship of marriage, must be examined in the context of Paul's distinctive call to all Christians—in all relationships—verse 21: "[Everyone is to be] subject to one another out of reverence for Christ." This is a general principle by which all Christians are to be guided. We are commanded, not just women, but all persons—men and women and children, masters and slaves—to live a life of submission. Not because of our station in life but because Jesus lived a life of submission and showed us that that's the only way to find life.

When we connect Paul's words to wives and husbands, we see no high and low positions in Christian marriage, or in the Christian community. A new order has been born, in which all participants regard themselves as servants of one master—Jesus Christ. We give ourselves in mutual service to one another because Christ modeled submission for us.

When we think of marriage in that fashion, we realize that *decision* and *intention* are essential. Marriage is more than feeling. The romantic love that we feel at the time we marry, which has a lot to do with physical attraction and sexual passion, may lose some of its zest. Our feelings may become numb, even confused. We get busy and preoccupied with the job, the kids, the church. Our commitment to our marriage may become vague, even distorted. Then, deep down in that mysterious abyss of ourselves, we begin to doubt—am I in love? Was I ever in love? Those are the wrong questions to ask. It's not a matter of *being in* love; it's a matter of *deciding to* love.

In marriage, we don't pledge to love as long as we feel good, as long as there is physical attraction and romantic response. We pledge to love for better, for worse, for richer, for poorer, in sickness, and in health. This vow wisely recognizes that feelings fluctuate. It also insists that we bring these fluctuations of feeling into the safe harbor of a love decision.

In that question the church asks of a couple being married, "Will you take this man/woman to be your wedded wife/husband?" the question is "Will you allow this decision to be an exclusive one that cancels out all other alternatives as long as life lasts?" Will you decide to keep on deciding to love?

EXPRESSED IN COMMITMENT

Love is decision, and marriage is commitment. It is more than a commitment to marriage as an institution, it is a commitment to our mate in marriage. Institutions are not sacred; persons are. It is easy to fall into the snare of commitment to an institution rather than to our marriage partner. I see it all the time. So the question is, "Are you committed?" And further, "What is the nature of your commitment? Is it to the institution of marriage or to your mate?"

If we understand marriage in this fashion, then "wives, be submissive to your husbands" should not fall heavily on the ears of women; and "husbands, love your wives as Christ loved the church and gave himself up for it" should not fall heavily on the ears of men. It is the Christian style of mutual submission.

QUESTIONS FOR REFLECTION

Spend some time reflecting on this claim: Love is decision; marriage is commitment. How does your relationship to Christ influence your relationship to your spouse? Have you loved your spouse and your family with Christlike love today?

30

DRY BONES AND AN EMPTY TOMB

LUKE 24:1-12; EZEKIEL 37:1-14

The Bible was written by different people at different times, in different places. The climactic message of the Bible, as a whole, is our salvation through Jesus Christ. We must be careful in seeking to interpret individual portions of Scripture apart from what John Wesley called the "whole scope and tenor of Scripture" (Sermon 110, "Free Grace").

There is a connection, in both image and meaning, between Ezekiel's vision in the valley of dry bones and the resurrection of Jesus. This famous vision of the valley of dry bones was given to Ezekiel shortly after the fall of Jerusalem to Babylonia in 587 B.C. The prophet is seized by "the hand of the Lord" (Ezek. 1:3 and 8:1) and sent into an ecstatic state in which he sees a new reality.

Israel was *dead* in exile. That is certainly the way she felt (cf. 33:10; Isaiah 53:8-9). The forces of death are overwhelming: she has lost her land, her temple, her Davidic king, her covenant, and her relationship with her God. In exile now, she is lifeless and without hope. Dry bones scattered about a parched and desolate valley are a graphic image of Israel's self-perception.

CAN THESE DRY BONES LIVE?

We have been there, haven't we? God's question to Ezekiel confronts us too. Ezekiel therefore hears the enigmatic question asked him by God, "Son of man, can these bones live?" (37:3 NIV). Life crumbles in on us, loving relationships are altered—diluted by misunderstanding or destroyed by unfaithfulness, lost by death. Evil stalks our streets, undermining trust of others and any sense of security. Violence and terrorism are rampant around the world, and we wonder if community goodness is even possible. The only answer we have is the answer of Ezekiel, "O Lord GOD, you know."

That must have been the mood of the women when they went to the tomb to anoint the body of Jesus. They had come with Jesus from Galilee. They had seen that awful crucifixion, the whipped body of Jesus nailed to the cross, the raising of that cross into the sun, and that loud, deadly thud settling it into an upright position. They heard his anguished cries; they saw the mocking of the crowd; and they watched the soldiers pierce his side. They witnessed the sweat flowing down his bloodstained face; they looked as he mustered all the energy that was left in his near-lifeless body to speak— to speak memorable words—words that they could never forget: "Father, forgive them for they know not what they do." "It is finished." "Father, into Thy hands I commit my Spirit."

They saw all that. But they also saw the nobility of a man named Joseph of Arimathea. He was a righteous man, looking for the Kingdom of God but still consenting to the decision of the council for the condemnation of Jesus. He didn't speak before, but he spoke now. He spoke because he couldn't let it rest there. He went to Pilot and asked for the body of Jesus. He took the body down from the cross and wrapped it in a linen shroud, and he laid Jesus in a rock-hewn tomb (Luke 23:50-56). Joseph came late to the Lord, but he came.

Because the Sabbath was beginning, the women couldn't do the normal preparation for burial, so they waited through the Sabbath day. And on the first day of the week, they went to the tomb. When they got to the tomb, with their spices to anoint Jesus' body, "They found the stone rolled away" (Luke 24:2). The women came late, but they still came.

That's the dramatic detail and metaphor connecting us with the valley of dry bones: "They found the stone rolled away." Let's use that metaphor to assist us in appropriating the powerful message of Easter. The stone was rolled away. The greatest affirmation of the church is not the affirmation that Jesus was born of the Virgin Mary. It's not the affirmation that he performed incredible miracles, or that he was a profound teacher, or that he embodied the very presence of God; but that he was crucified, dead, and buried, but rose and is alive today.

HOPE ALWAYS HAS THE LAST WORD

Return to Ezekiel. He was wise in answering the question from God, "Can these dry bones live?" with humility, yet with confidence: "O Lord GOD, you know." Human means are not sufficient to confront and overcome the forces of death that move in upon us almost daily. With our own power, we seem helpless to deal with broken relationships, suffering, crime, violence, and evil. The fact and the metaphor "the stone was rolled away" gives more powerful meaning to Ezekiel's message that only God can make an entire valley of dry bones come alive. Our bones are dried up. O God, will you restore us? Ezekiel is talking about the restoration and healing of our life here and now. And he is saying that only God can work that transformation.

The women made that discovery. When they arrived at the tomb, to their surprise and astonishment, *the stone was rolled away*. God had done it. The meaning in that phrase is expansive and empowering. Jesus is alive, and because of that, the stone of *defeat and despair is rolled away, making a way for hope*.

As humans, we have all known defeat. It doesn't help to hide that fact. The first step in moving beyond defeat is to admit and accept it for what it is.

94   *The Grace-Filled Life*

- *We have failed in friendship.* Sometimes by our anger and hostility but more often by our indifference we have let friends go. Or we have allowed differences to fester until the tie that bound us together is severed.
- *We have failed in marriage.* Some of the fault may be with our spouse, but in our most honest moments we know that at least a part of the trouble is within us. We have not been intentional in our expressions of love, allowing affection to grow cold. We may still be married, but the depth of love and the warmth of relationship is no longer there.
- *We have failed as parents.* Our children have not received what we sought to teach them about values, in part because our behavior has not matched our words. Their commitments are not our commitments, and it is difficult not to feel some guilt about this. We may even wonder about the depth of our faith when that faith is not replicated in our children's faith.

In so many other ways, we know about defeat. The message of the valley of dry bones and the resurrection of Jesus is that the stone of defeat and despair is rolled away, making a way for hope. But we can't connect the valley of dry bones and the resurrection too tightly. Ezekiel is not thinking and talking about bodily resurrection after death but restoration and healing of life in the here and now. But on this side of the resurrection of Jesus, we can't ignore that *the stone of death is rolled away, providing a doorway to eternal life with God.*

Return to Ezekiel again. In verses 11-14, the Lord interprets the vision for his prophet. Israel has been dead in exile; but like bodies being exhumed from the grave, Israel will be raised up once more by her Lord. She will return to her homeland, where she will be granted life and a future and hope anew (cf. Jer. 29:10-11). Israel is not "clean cut off," as she has believed (v. 11). She is not destined simply to wither away and die in a foreign land. God has not deserted her (cf. Isa. 40:27). Rather, he treasures her as the "apple of his eye" (Deut. 32:10) and loves her and will restore her to a good life.

Can these dead bones live? Some of us are as good as dead *spiritually*, conscious only of living out nine-to-five in what has been called "lives of quiet desperation." Some of us are as good as dead *morally* and live by the dictum, "If it feels good, we do it," despite the fact that we feel uneasy, even miserable, about the way we are living.

Can your bones live again? Yes, in Christ your Lord. The stone was rolled away and Christ, who came that you might have life and have it more abundantly, is alive to transform every valley of dry bones into life, hope, and joy.

What stones of past failure and sin need to be rolled away to give birth to hope? If you named one "dry bones" aspect or relationship in your life, what would it be? What is the primary barrier to joy in your life?

31

MIRACLES IN CONTRAST

LEVITICUS 23:23-32; 2 KINGS 23:21-27; JOHN 1:1-18

When the writer of the Gospel of John told the Christmas story, he didn't do it like Matthew and Luke did. He didn't talk about the Bethlehem drama with Mary and Joseph and the baby, angels singing, the shepherds and wise men following a star. Rather, John began to make some stupendous claims about the life and character of Jesus, the One who came at Christmastime. We almost hold our breath as we read that story, the atmosphere is so charged. Then we come to that mighty assertion in the fourth and fifth verses, and we have to stop and take a deep breath.

"In him was life, and the life was the light of all people. The light shines in the darkness, and the darkness did not overcome it" (John 1:4-5). There it is. The miracle in contrast. Light against darkness, and the darkness never snuffs it out. With that key, let's unlock the door of this passage from John's Gospel.

THE LIGHT THAT CANNOT BE OVERCOME

Life and light is the theme of John's Gospel. In the first chapter, he states the theme. Here at the beginning, we read that Jesus was *life*. And then at the very end, we read that John's aim in writing the Gospel was that people might believe that Jesus is the Christ, the son of God, and believing that, would have *life* through his name (John 20:31).

The word *life* is continually on the lips of Jesus. He defined his mission: "I came that they may have life, and have it abundantly" (10:10). He claims that he gives people life and that they will never perish because no one will pluck them out of his hand (10:28). His most expansive and radical claim was "I am the way, and the truth, and the life. No one comes to the Father but through me" (14:6). In the Gospel of John, the word *life* occurs more than thirty-five times and the verb *to live*, or *to have life*, more than thirteen times.

"In him was life, and the life was the *light* of all people" (emphasis added). That's the second of the great key words of John. This word *light* occurs no less than twenty-one times in John's Gospel. *Jesus*, John says, *is the light of men.* The mission of John the Baptist was to point persons to the light that was Christ. Twice Jesus calls himself the light of the world. This light can be in people so that they can become children of the light. "I am come," Jesus said, "a light unto the world" (John 12:46 KJV). This is the meaning of Christ's coming— the great miracle in contrast: *light and life set against death and darkness.*

The seed miracle in contrast is this: human babe, divine incarnation. Ask a Buddhist, a Hindu, or a Muslim—you might even ask a Jew—what he or she thinks about God being born a baby. Ask any devotee of a religion other than Christianity what they think of a God who would come to earth in a little baby. After a while, it may begin to dawn on you that this is the pivotal truth of Christianity. No one has captured this more grippingly than Robert Southwell, the religious poet of the sixteenth century.

> This little babe a few days old is come to rival Satan's fold.
> All hell doth at his presence quake, though he himself for cold do shake.
> For in this weak, unarmed wise, the gates of hell he will surprise.

Isn't that what we desperately long for, deep down at the center of our being? We need to know that God has come to us and has identified himself completely with our life. It really doesn't help us too much to know that there is a God somewhere—or to be told any number of nice things about him, until we know that the cold blasts of wind that shake us, shake him.

There is a cold wind of impersonality that blows through the business and social worlds where we all live. We watch it strike our friends and their families—jobs are lost, hope is shattered. Friends turn cold, and we feel left outside circles where we thought we were included. We go to our rooms at night and look out on the lights of the city: people pass, but they don't look. A thirty-five-year-old dies of cancer and a seventeen-year-old is killed in an auto accident. Dare we believe that the God of the universe "himself for cold do shake"? It would help if we could, wouldn't it?

Listen to those texts that dramatically punctuate the Gospel and you'll see who God is and the meaning of the coming of Christ.

> For God, who commanded the light to shine out of darkness, hath shined in our hearts. (2 Cor. 4:6 KJV)

> In him was life, and the life was the light of all people. (John 1:4)

Human babe, divine incarnation.

It is from this miracle in contrast that we give joyous witness to other miracles that ensue. *There is the dark night of sin and guilt, broken in upon by the bright dawn of forgiveness and acceptance.* It comes with the ultimate expression of love as Jesus gives himself for our redemption on the Cross.

In the Old Testament, the Passover and the Day of Atonement were efforts to respond to this deepest of all needs. The Passover is one of the most vivid stories in the Old Testament. What the crucifixion is for Christians, the Passover is for Israel. The firstborn of Israel were spared by the sprinkling of the blood of a lamb on the doorposts, identifying them as those who had heard God's call and were faithful.

> For I will pass through the land of Egypt that night, and I will strike down every firstborn in the land of Egypt, both human beings and animals; on all the gods of Egypt I will execute judgments: I am the LORD. The blood shall be a sign for you on the houses where you live: when I see the blood, I will pass over you, and no plague shall destroy you when I strike the land of Egypt. (Exod. 12:12-13)

From then until now, Jews have celebrated Passover as God's action of forgiveness and deliverance. Our scripture from 2 Kings is the account of King Josiah reinstating the Passover Feast in the life of the nation. For seventy-five years there had been no Passover feast held in Jerusalem, and even before that the ceremony had been diluted and revised to fit the whims of the rulers. With the rediscovery of the Law and the renewal of the covenant, the Passover once again had a central place in the life of Israel.

It is not a long leap in reflection to connect Passover with the Cross. The Lord had said, "The blood will be a sign," or "token" as some translations have it. It was the token of redemption at the Passover—and now, how much more so, is the crucifixion for Christians.

ARMED WITH THE POWER OF LOVE ALONE

In Christ on the cross, God speaks that forgiving word and here again is the miracle in contrast—dark night of sin and guilt, bright dawn of forgiveness and acceptance. What a strategy on the part of God! It is nothing less than taking hell by storm. What is the focus here? Another miracle in contrast. Strong powers of physical strength, military might, intellectual acumen, economic power—in contrast to the weak Son, submissive to the Father, armed only with love as a weapon. "Father, forgive them; for they do not know what they are doing" (Luke 23:34). Here is the strongest power in heaven and on Earth—nothing but love. That's the reason the gates of hell are taken by surprise.

When the cold wind of impersonality blows through the world where we live, what warms us? Love. When those we love the most choose the far country and we can do nothing but wait, what gives us the strength to continue hoping? Love. Miracles in contrast—our Passover and our Day of Atonement is every day, so let the text say it again. "In him appeared life, and that life was the light of mankind. The light still shines in the darkness, and the darkness has never put it out" (John 1:5 GNT).

QUESTIONS FOR REFLECTION

What do you think about God being born a baby? How is Christ as life and light impacting your daily life? What are the signs in your community that Christ is surprising "the gates of hell"? If there are no signs, why?

32

SAMARIA AND OUR SPIRITUAL JOURNEY

DANIEL 3:8-28; JOHN 4:1-15

Edward de Bono is regarded by many to be the leading authority in the world in the field of creative thinking and the direct teaching of thinking as a skill. He is the originator of lateral thinking. He illustrated what he means by lateral thinking in an experience he had as a Rhodes Scholar in Oxford. One night he attended a party in London. The party ended late, and he got back to Oxford after the gates were closed. In order to get to his room, he had to scale the college walls. There were two walls. He got over the first one, came to the second, climbed and jumped down on the other side only to find himself outside again. He had climbed in and out across a corner of the wall.

He tried again—this time with more attention to where the second wall was. He noticed that there was a gate in the wall, and as the gate was lower than the rest of the wall, and provided foot holes, he decided to climb over the gate. He did, and as he was sitting astride the top of the gate, it slowly opened. It had never been locked.

He learned a lesson: no matter how good you are in climbing a wall, you should always pick the right one. When he applied that to problem solving, he called it "lateral thinking." Instead of facing problems head-on, try looking at them from another angle. Don't attack head-on: take detours, moving laterally, or even sometimes backward, until you find the gate that no one knew was open.

That is a good way to reflect on Scripture. I have applied it to my study on the familiar stories of Jesus and the woman at the well and of Shadrach, Meshach, and Abednego in the fiery furnace.

There are obvious lessons in our passage from John 4: the breaking down of barriers is a central lesson, as is the universal presence of God. There is the monumental lesson in Jesus' radical claim that he is the source of meaning in life: "Everyone who drinks of this water will be thirsty again, but those who drink of the water that I will give them will never be thirsty" (4:13).

SAMARIA IN OUR LIVES

But do some lateral thinking. Back away from the story; move in and out of it; take some detours in thinking; look from the side rather than head-on and you can see that, first, there is a Samaria in all our lives. Second, there is a ministry in Samaria. And third, Samaria is something we *pass through*, not stay in.

There is a Samaria in all our lives. "Jesus had to go through Samaria" (v. 4). He could have gone another way; most Jews did.

The land of Palestine included Galilee in the extreme North, Judea was in the South; and in between, Samaria. The journey from Judea to Galilee could be done in three days if you went straight through Samaria. The alternate route was to cross the Jordan River down in Judea, go up the eastern side of the river without passing through Samaria, then recross the Jordan north of Samaria and enter Galilee there. This alternative route took twice as long. Jews took the longer route because they hated the Samaritans and did not want to be contaminated by them. But for Jesus, it wasn't the timing or the distance, rather, it was who he was that he "had to pass through Samaria."

I remember counseling with a man who was struggling with a decision about work. He was connected with a company that was deeply involved in the gambling business. My friend was torn to pieces inside because he could not bear to be identified with that part of the company. It violated his moral sensitivities and called into question his Christian commitment. He was wrestling with how to disengage himself. He was in the middle of Samaria.

At one time or another, there is a Samaria in each of our lives. For Shadrach, Meshach, and Abednego it was as dramatic as possible. Their Samaria was in Babylon. They had been made administrators under King Nebuchadnezzar. Their position made other officials jealous. So these officials made themselves enemies of Shadrach, Meshach, and Abednego, and reported to the king that these Hebrews were not serving the Babylonian gods and were not bowing and worshiping the golden statue as the king had commanded. Nebuchadnezzar called the boys into his court to question them. Here they made a beautiful response. They said, in effect, "O King, we offer no defense. If you throw us into the furnace, our God is able to save us." Then comes one of richest statements of faith in the Bible, "But even if [God] does not, we want you to know, O king, that we will not serve your gods or worship the image of gold" (Dan. 3:18 NIV). Babylon was their Samaria.

But *Samaria is not just a place, it is an experience.* For some it is the fact of an illness, pronounced incurable. For another it is the early death of a spouse, and for another a new life of single motherhood because of divorce. It may be a rebellious child or the trying ordeal of living with an addictive spouse. Sooner or later, most of us will have to pass through some Samaria in our lives.

MINISTRY IN SAMARIA

A second truth from our lateral thinking is there is a ministry in Samaria. If we keep faith, stay alert, and keep our eyes, ears, and hearts open, we will find a ministry in our Samaria. Jesus discovered this at Jacob's well in his encounter with the Samaritan woman. She came to the well in the middle of the day to get water.

And for one time in her life, this woman with the tangled and tired and tinged history found someone who would care enough to treat her with respect. Jesus engaged her in conversation, listened to her, and loved her with an uncondemning love.

In the story of the three Hebrew boys, when they refused to compromise their faith, Nebuchadnezzar had a temper tantrum. He ordered that the furnace be heated seven times hotter than usual and the boys be thrown into it. The furnace was so hot that the flames killed several soldiers who were tossing the boys into it. Through a bottom door in the furnace, where fuel and air were introduced, the king could see what was happening. To his amazement, the boys were walking around, unhurt. He was shocked. When the boys were brought out of the furnace, not a hair of their heads had been singed. Not only that, but there seemed to be four people in the furnace, not three. There was not even the smell of smoke on them. In verse 29 the king praised the God of Shadrach, Meshach, and Abednego who rescued them. He said, "No other god can save in this way." Then he gave them a promotion. In the fiery trials of Babylon, Shadrach, Meshach, and Abednego served God and performed a ministry.

It doesn't matter where our Samaria is, there is a ministry there.

Now this final lesson: *on our spiritual journey, our Samaria is to pass through, not to stay in.* It doesn't help to try to explain our Samaria or to rationalize it. It is debilitating to take a burden of guilt upon ourselves because we are in Samaria. Most of all, it doesn't help to try to fix blame, especially to blame God for our Samaria. It does help to know that we are not meant to stay in Samaria; God will give us the grace to pass *through.*

It makes all the difference in the world how we face our Samaria or our fiery furnace. We can face it with fear and trembling and be left impotent. We can ignore the fact that we are there, closing our eyes to the circumstances, failing to acknowledge that closing our eyes only leaves us blind. We can live passively in Samaria and be consumed by the forces of it. Or we can face it freely in faith, know that "this too will pass," but while we are there we are going to find a ministry and be Christ to those we meet in Samaria.

QUESTIONS FOR REFLECTION

What does it mean that Samaria is not a place but an experience? Are you in Samaria now? Have you found a ministry there? What gives you the courage and strength to pass through Samaria?

33

"THAT'S GOOD FOR WHAT AILS YOU"

PSALM 96:1-6, 11-13; PROVERBS 17:14-22

The Bible is a serious book, but it is not deadly serious. Have you ever thought we might have been better off if we had never printed the Bible between black covers? In his novel *The Brothers Karamazov*, Dostoevsky characterized the artificial life of the monastery as "twenty-five men trying to be saints, who sit around looking blankly at each other and eat cabbage." That kind of attitude toward the Christian life and the Bible is too prevalent and takes away from the seriousness of the whole matter.

It took me a while in my Christian journey to realize that to be a serious Christian didn't mean that I had to go around looking like I had been baptized in lemon juice. To be a serious Christian meant that I needed to be happy, joyful, full of cheer. I titled the most autobiographical book I've ever written *Dancing at My Funeral*.

ABUNDANT JOY, ABUNDANT LIVING

So, I repeat so you won't miss it. The Bible is a serious book but not deadly serious. It's a book that calls us to life, abundant life; to joy that no one can take away. It's a book that calls God's people to celebrate, to clap their hands and shout for joy.

The 96th Psalm begins with a word that punctuates so many of the Psalms, "Sing to the LORD a new song; / sing to the LORD, all the earth." The expansiveness of singing joy is expressed in exultation:

Let the heavens be glad, and let the earth rejoice;
 let the sea roar, and all that fills it; . . .
Then shall all the trees of the forest sing for joy
 before the LORD. (vv. 11-13)

The Proverbs, likewise, are punctuated with this call to happiness and joy, emphasizing what robs us of joy as much as what provides it. A case in point in verse 14 of our selected reading from Proverbs 17: "The beginning of strife is like letting out water; / so stop before the quarrel breaks out." The classic call to joy, which we quote all the time, is in this chapter, verse 22: "A cheerful heart is a good medicine, / but a downcast spirit dries up the bones."

The entire collection of Proverbs is punctuated with this claim of the renewing, even healing and transforming, power of "a cheerful heart." There are two verses in Proverbs 15 that are vivid expressions of it. "A glad heart makes a cheerful countenance, / but by sorrow of heart the spirit is broken" (v. 13). "All the days of the poor are hard, / but a cheerful heart has a continual feast" (v. 15). This ancient writer knew what it has taken medical science a long time to discover—laughter is a healing medicine for soul and body.

LAUGH TILL IT HELPS

Norman Cousins was one of the most outstanding journalists of the twentieth century. For years he was the editor of the *Saturday Review*. His lifelong concerns were large and varied: world peace, world governance, justice, human freedom, the human impact on the environment, and health and wholeness. During a lifetime that spanned most of the twentieth century, these central concerns of Cousins's life were also among the most important issues facing the human race.

In the 1960s Cousins had an experience that changed his life. He wrote about it in a book entitled *Anatomy of an Illness*. In 1964 he was flying home from an overseas meeting and felt a fever coming on. In the hospital, his situation was diagnosed as a kind of arthritic degenerative disease. The prognosis was paralysis for the rest of his life at best and, at worst, death. The longer he was in the hospital and the more medication he took, the worse he got. Finally he asked his doctor, who was also a good friend, if he could experiment with some rather unorthodox therapy. The doctor reluctantly agreed. Cousins's request was threefold: first, to leave the hospital and check into a hotel room across the street; second, to stop all drugs and to take massive doses of vitamin C; and finally, to be allowed to view comedy films. Alan Funt was a good friend of Norman Cousins, and he supplied hours and hours of old videotapes of *Candid Camera*. The doctor agreed to all this, and the results were immediate, and in no time, Cousins was dramatically better.

There is considerable controversy over what happened, but the fact is Norman Cousins was cured of a dreadful disease. And at least he believed that laughter had a great deal to do with his recovery. He said that laughter was able to do for his body what drugs were supposed to do but couldn't. Laughter relaxed him so that he could sleep at night. Laughter changed his attitude so that he was optimistic about the future. And laughter seemed to encourage his body's own intrinsic recuperative powers.

The evidence is becoming more and more convincing. Our attitudes contribute to our sickness, our dis-ease—but also to our healing. But not only do laughter and cheerfulness provide medicine for the physical life, they are medicine for our minds, our emotions, our spirits, our relationships. They are medicine for the whole self.

We are talking about the medicine of cheerfulness. So let's use happiness as a rubric to guide our reflection. Having expressed these convictions, it may sound strange to affirm that *I need to be able to be happy that I am unhappy.* A lot of thinking and talking about happiness is superficial, and I don't want to fall into that snare. So register my affirmation, which I hope will become yours. I'm happy that I can be unhappy. There are many, many reasons for us to be unhappy, and we need to confess that.

One of the dimensions of being human is that we have the capacity to feel beyond ourselves—to feel the pain of others, to register the joys but also the sorrows of a world beyond our personal experience. Poverty, homelessness, little children starving, Palestinians fighting Israelis, residents in urban settings being victimized by gangs, friends getting a divorce, parents grieving over losing a child to the dark world of drugs. These things make me unhappy, and I'm happy that I am unhappy, that my heart is heavy with sadness in relation to these issues.

Hopefully, registering this will give more depth and seriousness to my next affirmations. *I'm happy that I can be happy with myself.* I doubt if anything will be a more healing medicine for any one of us than to be happy in celebrating ourselves. Jesus valued us; why can't we value ourselves?

This final thought: *I'm happy that my happiness does not depend on circumstance.* Did you note the order of one of our proverbs? "A cheerful heart has a continual feast" follows the statement, "All the days of the poor are hard." Our biggest problem is our attitudes toward our problems. No one can deny that we have almost unbelievable problems that we think are unsolvable. We have problems in our city. We have personal problems: illness, loneliness, death of loved ones, threatened divorce, loss of jobs. Even so, I contend our biggest problem is our attitudes toward our problems. I'm happy that my happiness does not depend on circumstance. I can determine my attitude toward my circumstance.

A young Jewish girl in the Warsaw Ghetto managed to escape over the wall and hide in a cave. She died shortly before the Allied Army liberated the Ghetto. Before she died, however, she had scratched on the wall three things that were her living witness to the world. In that depressing, dangerous, life-threatening situation, this is what she wrote: "I believe in the sun, even when it is not shining." "I believe in love, even when feeling it not." "I believe in God, even when God is silent" (*Pulpit Digest*, December, 1970, p. 58).

In Perry County, Mississippi, where I grew up, we had a saying: "That's good for what ails you." Laughter, happiness, and a cheerful heart is that kind of medicine.

QUESTIONS FOR REFLECTION

What are you happy about today? What are you happy to not be happy about? Who needs you to bring joy into their lives?

34

HOSEA: A LIVING SERMON

HOSEA 3:1-5, 6:1-6; JOHN 8:1-11

At different times through the years I have practiced a discipline I call *being quiet before the Word*. It is a way of using meditation and imagination to pray and receive the message of God through Scripture. I center down, deliberately putting myself in the presence of God. I seek to be what I call *passively open* as I read a passage of Scripture. I don't try to figure things out or impose rational thought or logic, but I listen to the Scripture speak. I make whatever application to my life that seems appropriate and deal with the feelings that come, seeking to make the word my own.

This practice is most meaningful when I write—either spontaneously or deliberately, recording my thoughts and feelings. On an occasion when I was living with Hosea in this devotional fashion, I came to Hosea 3:1: "Go, love a woman who . . . is an adulteress." I sought to put myself in Hosea's place,

What?
  Love this woman who has shattered my heart into splinters?
  Love this woman who has played the harlot?
  Do you know what you are asking, God?
  How many nights have I cried myself to sleep?
  How many evenings have I fumbled
      to explain to three anxious children
      the mystery of no mother at home?
  How many anguished hours have I tried
      to cool and caress to peace
      the fevered brow of children
      who needed the mother's touch?
  How many midnights have I contorted in passion
      my loins aching for the satisfaction of a woman
      my mind ablaze with the rage of knowing
          my woman was soothing the fiery desires of another man?
  What are you saying, God?
      "Go again, love this woman who has played the harlot?"
  You can't mean it!
  You do?
  And why?
      "Even as the Lord loves the people of Israel

> though they turn to other gods
>   and love cakes of raisins."
> Only for you, God—only for you!

Hosea is one of the most intriguing books in the Bible because the prophet himself became a "living sermon."

A LIVING SERMON

God instructed Hosea to marry his wife, Gomer, who had been a harlot. After bearing three children, she returned to her life of shame, "playing the harlot . . . going after lovers . . . burning incense to Baal." We can only imagine the pain and despair of Hosea, the throbbing ache of his soul. Yet the shock of it all is not in what Gomer had done but in Hosea hearing God's command, "Go, love a woman who . . . is an adulteress" (Hos. 3:1).

To live out the message of God, who is the lover of those who are not worthy of his love, the prophet brought back his wayward wife. She was not worthy of his love—but we don't love because of "worthiness"—nor was Israel worthy of God's love. Israel had gone after other gods as Gomer went after other men.

God's love would not let Israel go. Are there more tender words in all Scripture than these?

> When Israel was a child, I loved him,
>   and out of Egypt I called my son. . . .
> I led them with cords of human kindness,
>   with bands of love. . . .
> How can I give you up, Ephraim?
>   How can I hand you over, O Israel? (Hos. 11:1, 4, 8)

When I read Hosea it reminds me also of the New Testament story of the woman caught in the act of adultery (John 8). Gomer was a guilty whore, as guilty as the woman the Pharisees brought to Jesus to test him concerning the law that adulterers were to be stoned. Neither woman deserved love and forgiveness, yet both received them.

Two things stand out in Jesus' response to the woman. One, *the privilege of judgment belongs to God, not to us*. Jesus refused to allow the woman's accusers to pass judgment. He was forthright in his command, "Do not judge, so that you may not be judged" (Matt. 7:1). Two, *if we are to break the negative cycle of sin and evil, our first action must be merciful action for redemption, not punishment or retaliation*. Jesus' answer to sin and the pervasive power of evil was radical love and forgiveness.

In all our relationships and in our response to circumstances around us, we need to ask ourselves questions like these: Are we more interested in judgment than mercy? Are we more committed to punishment than redemption? The story of Jesus and the woman caught in adultery turns on Jesus' statement to her accusers: "Let anyone among you who is without sin be the first to throw a stone at her" (John 8:7).

WHY SO DIFFICULT?

Bring that home. Look at your relationships and the events of your life during the past few months. Have you experienced some jealousy that prevented you from celebrating the success of someone you know, maybe even a loved one? Have you refused to accept the word of another as truth because you still harbor the memory of a lie that person told you? Have you kept alive a morsel of destructive gossip? Have you secretly delighted in the misfortune of another? Are you still bearing a grudge against someone who did you wrong, though that one has sought to make amends? Is there still a small fire of resentment burning inside because you've not forgiven the one who stole some happiness from you and caused you pain?

Why is it so easy to judge and condemn, and so difficult to love and forgive when we know that is the way of redemption? This story reinforces the consistent theme of John's Gospel, the theme climactically stated in John 3:16-17: "God so loved the world . . . God sent not his Son into the world to condemn the world; but that the world through him might be saved" (KJV). We don't know the total situation of the woman accused of adultery. Whatever the case, Jesus' admonition, "go and sin no more" (John 8:11 KJV), is his way of giving the woman another chance. That's the New Testament emphasis on forgiveness that Hosea demonstrated so powerfully.

QUESTIONS FOR REFLECTION

Are your secret delights also delightful to God? Is there still a small fire of resentment burning inside of you that needs the salve of forgiveness? Is there a pattern of punishment and retaliation in your family or in your larger community that needs to be broken by merciful actions of redemption?

35

THE MINISTRY OF UNBINDING

JOHN 11:38-44

Somewhere along the way I heard this definition of Christian obedience:

A Christian is a *mind* through which Christ *thinks*;
A *heart* through which Christ *loves*;
A *voice* through which Christ *speaks*;
A *hand* through which Christ *helps*.

I think of that as I begin to reflect on one of the most well-known, tender, and challenging stories in the New Testament: Jesus raising Lazarus. It hits me right off: *we cannot raise people from the dead as Jesus did, but we share in the deliverance of those he has raised.* Death—and what is done about that—is in Jesus' hands. It is he who can say with power, "Come out!" But deliverance—that's in our hands. "Unbind him," Jesus said. "Unbind him, and let him go" (John 11:44).

UNBOUND TO LIFE WITH JESUS

The story is packed with invitation and challenge. *Love is here.* "Jesus loved Martha and her sister and Lazarus" (v. 5). Faith is here. Both Mary and Martha said the same thing to Jesus at different points in the story. "Lord, if you had been here, my brother would not have died" (vv. 21, 32). *Compassion is here.* When Jesus saw Mary and her friend weeping, "he was deeply moved in spirit and troubled"; he offered compassion that was tender with tears: "Jesus wept" (vv. 33, 35 NIV). Apart from the raising of Lazarus, perceptive teaching is there. "If anyone walks in the day, he does not stumble, because he sees the light of the world. But if anyone walks in the night, he stumbles because the light is not in him" (vv. 9-10). Climaxing it all, *power is here.* "Lazarus, come out!" The dead man came out (v. 41).

We could focus anywhere in that lineup of the ingredients of this astounding story, but let's center on two details in the story, which, on first blush, may appear incidental. Jesus came to the tomb, a cave, and a stone was lying against it. Jesus said, "Take away the stone" (vv. 38-39)—a matter-of-fact request. Have you ever wondered why Jesus didn't make it even more dramatic? Why he didn't do something like God did with the veil of the Temple on the day of the Crucifixion—rend it in two? If he could raise a man who had been dead for four days, why would he handle the stone in such a mundane fashion, calling the men to take it away?

Could it be that where human power is sufficient, divine power will not come forth? I know it may be a surprising thought, and what follows may be more surprising. *Is it possible to be too dependent upon God?*

I'm not offering the gospel as support for an insensitive philosophy to "pull yourself up by your own bootstraps." The problem with that philosophy is that there are too many who don't have boots, so there are no straps to pull on. I know full well that the message of the gospel is that God helps those who are helpless—not just the *down-and-out* helpless, but, like so many of us, the *up-and-out* helpless. Yet I still pose the question: Is it possible to be too dependent upon God? Though extreme, the question makes the previous statement clearer: Where human power is sufficient, divine power will not come forth.

Another way to talk about this notion is to say that Christ has great respect for us as human instruments in his Kingdom enterprise. Jesus said, "Take away the stone." He uses us as instruments for his work.

THE MINISTRY OF UNBINDING

The second detail of the Lazarus story is equally challenging. We move from the height of miraculous glory—the raising of a dead man—to the down-to-earth task of releasing Lazarus from his grave clothes so that he might be free. "Unbind him, and let him go."

We are called to a ministry of unbinding. There are people all around us, living with us in our families, laboring with us in our jobs, attending the same church, interacting with us as a part of our social networks, who have never experienced the resurrection power of Jesus Christ. They have heard and accepted the saving word of Christ—"Come forth"—but they are still bound and need to be delivered. Their grave-bindings are diverse and yet, sadly, common.

- *Low Self-esteem*: perhaps a common psychological problem, yet it is a serious spiritual disease, which can be healed by love and attention.
- *Prejudice*: a destructive mindset that values ourselves more than others and produces destructive action, which can be altered by our speaking the truth in love and demonstrating the inherent value of all God's children.
- *Guilt and shame*: the cumulative burden of unconfessed sin or the imposition of stringent expectations that are never met, some of which could

never be met, all of which can be "unbound" by forgiveness—our forgiveness, which communicates the forgiveness of Christ.

QUESTIONS FOR REFLECTION

In what way might you be too dependent on God? What keeps you tied to your past? Who is Jesus calling you to unbind?

36

"IF ONLY . . . IN SPITE OF"

2 TIMOTHY 4:9-18; NUMBERS 13:25-33

Do the following names have any meaning to you? *Shammua, Shaphat, Igal, Palti, Gaddiel, Gaddi, Ammiel, Sethur, Nahbi, Geuel.* Those are the first names of the spies who were sent out with Joshua and Caleb to investigate the land and determine whether Israel could possess Canaan.

LIVING THE "IF ONLY" LIFE

One group was sent out, but two reports came back. There was a majority and a minority report. The majority report, made by the individuals mentioned above, reflected fear and weakness, lack of faith and courage: "We are not able to go up against this people, for they are stronger than we. . . . There we saw the Nephilim [giants]; and to ourselves we seemed like grasshoppers, and so we seemed to them" (Numbers 13:31, 33). Joshua and Caleb had another perception: "Let us go up at once and occupy it, for we are well able to overcome it" (v. 30). The majority minimized God and maximized the giants. Their God was too weak, and they were too small; the task was too difficult, and the giants were too big.

The majority represent what I call an "if only" approach to life. Joshua and Caleb's response was an "in spite of" response. The majority would say, "if only" we had more troops, "if only" there were not so many of those giants, "if only" the cities were not so strongly fortified. They were frightened out of their minds, and their fear magnified the obstacles. "If only" leads to a grasshopper mentality.

Joshua and Caleb did not minimize the strength of the enemy or diminish the difficulty that would be encountered. "The people who live in the land are strong, and the towns are fortified and very large; and besides [there are giants] there" (v. 28). "In spite of" all that, we can overcome and possess the land.

There are two immediate lessons in the story. One, when you focus on fear instead of faith, you develop a grasshopper mentality. You become less than you are, and far less than is possible. Two, majority reports do not always provide the vision worth our following, so we need to be careful about taking our cue from the crowd.

The Grace-Filled Life

There is something very sad yet very exciting about our Scripture lesson in 2 Timothy. It was written at a time when survival was paramount in Paul's mind. He is an old man now; he's in prison; and he's about to be executed. But not only is there the question about his own personal survival, there is a question about the survival of the church itself. The churches that had been established didn't have buildings or budgets or staffs or status. For the most part, they were small gatherings of believers, meeting undercover in many places, under the threat of persecution and even annihilation.

Note Paul's description of the constituency of that early church:

> Consider your own call, brothers and sisters: not many of you were wise by human standards, not many were powerful, not many were of noble birth. But God chose what is foolish in the world to shame the wise; God chose what is weak in the world to shame the strong; God chose what is low and despised in the world, things that are not, to reduce to nothing things that are, so that no one might boast in the presence of God. (1 Cor. 1:26-29)

So, when Paul comes to write his letters to Timothy, there is every reason to wonder whether this thing called the church would survive much longer. Things didn't get better; they got worse. By the time the apostle John was taken off into captivity out of Ephesus to the island of Patmos, every observer of the human scene would have laid bets on the fact that Caesar, not Christ, had all the power.

So our Scripture lesson from 2 Timothy comes out of what by all human standards should have been the depths of despair. That is not the case. Loneliness and suffering and sadness are certainly there, but not despair. Do you feel it? Paul begs Timothy, "Do your best to come to me soon." Paul is in prison, almost totally alone; only Luke is with him. He wants Timothy to bring Mark with him and to bring his cloak, which he had left back in Troas. He also wants his books and parchment.

Verse 16 is packed with pathos. "At my first defense no one came to my support, but all deserted me." So there is sadness here, loneliness—but there is also an affirmation of tremendous faith and hope. "But the Lord stood by me and gave me strength, so that through me the message might be fully proclaimed and all the Gentiles might hear it. So I was rescued from the lion's mouth" (v. 17).

All the doors seemed to be closed—"if only," Paul could have dejectedly declared. Not so. For Paul something will open "in spite of," because "the Lord will rescue me from every evil attack and save me for His heavenly Kingdom. To him be the glory for ever and ever. Amen" (v. 18). Paul knew what we need to learn—that power is never ours with an "if only" attitude. But when we claim God's presence and promise, life can be abundantly rich "in spite of."

GOD IS NOT GOING TO LEAVE US

Trusting God, we soon learn that *in our brokenness we are forced to acknowledge our humanity, and in our suffering we discover our power.* So our brokenness can be the occasion when we are forced to acknowledge our humanity and turn to the source of help, Jesus Christ.

Don't miss the second part of the truth: in our suffering we *discover our power.* Vibrant Christian living lies not in eliminating troubles or problems but in growing with them. When problems come, we can curse God or we can waste our time in self-centeredness—throwing a big pity party and immersing ourselves in the energy-draining "if only" syndrome. We can center all of our thinking on the distorted notion that life is unfair—especially, unfair to us. Life is unfair—of course it is. But are we going to allow that fact to be the primary factor shaping our lives?

When I was a pastor in Memphis, we had a Sunday evening healing service. It was a time of spiritual centeredness—a time when the power of God was vividly evident. A big part of the service was prayer, prayer that centered in the celebration of Holy Communion—but also prayer that was shared in a special way with people who came to the altar where they could invite one of the ministers to be with them in their struggle, in their suffering, in their confusion, in their pain, in their deep concern about someone else.

I remember praying with a woman whom I had not known personally. She came and shared the fact that her daughter had died of AIDS, and she was wrestling with the pain of that—wrestling with her relationship with God and her understanding of God in light of the fact that her daughter had died in such a tragic, senseless way. We prayed and cried together—yes, I cried with her. One of the things that she said two or three times as we closed our prayer and I anointed her with oil was "God is not going to leave us, is he. God is not going to leave us, is he."

It was not a question but an affirmation—an affirmation we can all make. That's the reason we do not live paralyzed by the "if only" syndrome. We live "in spite of" because God is not going to leave us.

QUESTIONS FOR REFLECTION

Recall an occasion of brokenness and suffering when you discovered power and meaning. How can what you learned in that experience be applied to daily living? Do you have an "if only" faith or an "in spite of" faith?

37

ANOTHER COUNSELOR

JOHN 16:4-11; JOHN 17:1-5

It was the day before his crucifixion. Jesus may not have known it was going to be the day, but he knew it would be soon. He called his disciples together to celebrate Passover. There in the Upper Room, he rehearsed and reiterated his teaching, underscoring the most important lessons.

SO MUCH TO TEACH, SO LITTLE TIME

The Twelve were attached to Jesus, perhaps with the exception of Judas. They admired and respected him. They believed he was the Messiah. Though not always understanding, they marveled at his teaching. They were astonished at his power of healing and his power over nature. How could it be, they must have been asking themselves, that he was going away? Where was he going, and what would happen to them if he left them?

And this was the cause of sorrow at the Last Supper. They were saddened by Jesus' announcement of departure. The more he spoke about the future, the more confused they became, and the more fear and anxiety filled their minds. He could see it in their faces, and he acknowledged it, "You have pain now; but I will see you again, and your hearts will rejoice" (John 16:22). He has talked about it before, but now it comes as an astonishing, mind-boggling promise. "It is to your advantage that I go away, for if I do not go away, the Advocate will not come to you; but if I go, I will send him to you" (16:7).

The Advocate is the Holy Spirit, and Jesus tells them the Spirit will lead them into the truth. This word may not have clarified their confusion, but it gave the disciples the hope they desperately needed. Later they would experience what he was saying and in reflection they would understand, but at that moment it was beyond comprehension.

The Spirit would come and would speak with the authority of God, telling the disciples what God was thinking. The Spirit would give Jesus glory because he would translate what Jesus had to say to the disciples. Jesus tells them he possesses all the Father has, and he and the Father are one.

At best, the disciples grasped only a bit of it. Understandably so. How could they concentrate on such radical assertions when they had just been told what was going to happen? How could it happen to the one they thought would establish his Kingdom? And what about their part in all this? The fact that they didn't understand is clear when we read that Pentecost came as a shattering surprise.

After two thousand years, the coming of the Spirit is still a surprise. Most of us are not willing, much less ready, for the Holy Spirit to make us different, to change us, to empower us, to lead us. We try to put our faith into action without thought of an Advocate to be alongside us. We wrestle with problems, ideas, and intellectual dilemmas, forgetting the primary work of the Spirit is to guide us into truth. God has given his children their own personal Guide. "When the Spirit of truth comes, he will guide you into all the truth" (16:13). The word *guide* in the Greek language is a word that is used to describe someone who guides a person who is blind. It literally means "lead the way."

Looming through Jesus' incredible rehearsal and reiteration of his teaching are two monumental truths. First, he reminded them that they would suffer, that the world was and would be in turmoil, but that God's love and grace would triumph, and that he, Jesus, would be with them forever: "In the world you have tribulation; but be of good cheer, I have overcome the world" (16:33 RSV).

The Greek word that is translated "Advocate" or "Counselor" is *Paraclete*; it means the "one who takes our part, the one called alongside to help," but not only alongside, also within—in union with us as Christ is in union with God. Jesus' death and resurrection, making way for the coming of the Spirit, *revolutionizes our praying*. We know that we are loved by the Father as the Father loved Jesus. With the Spirit as an ongoing Presence, we are in the presence of the Father and the Son. In this intimate relationship, our prayer is Jesus' prayer. "Until now you have not asked for anything in my name. Ask and you will receive, so that your joy may be complete" (John 16:24). When we have the name of Jesus, we have the heart of God.

Jesus' death and resurrection, making way for the coming of the Spirit, *guarantees peace in tribulation*. That peace is possible because, united with Christ, we share his victory over the world.

The second monumental truth in Jesus' rehearsal and reiteration of his teaching is promise of eternal life. "This is eternal life, that they may know you, the only true God, and Jesus Christ whom you have sent" (17:3). There are two ways of looking at this—or maybe it's just two sides of the same coin. One is the promise of resurrection now: "This is eternal life." That's present tense, and when Jesus said, "Because I live, you also will live" (14:19), that's present tense as well. When we look at it this way, the proof of the Resurrection is not the empty tomb but the incredible transformation in the lives of the disciples. That's a matter of record. They remained ordinary men after the Resurrection, but they began to live extraordinary lives. Something had happened to them—something had come over them—they were living the Resurrection now.

I could tell you story after story of people who are living that kind of faith. A mother rears two children alone; but in her loneliness and frustration, she is sustained by a presence and power not her own. An alcoholic who lives one day at a time in commitment to Christ and celebrates this week eleven years of sobriety after far more years than that in hopeless despair. A young man who fights desperately a pitched battle with drug addiction, and praise God, by his dependency upon Christ, is winning the battle.

Then there are the countless ones whose stories are not so dramatic. They cope with fear and depression, the pressure of a demanding job, the energy-draining calls upon their lives as parents, teenagers who are refusing to let the world around them squeeze them into its mold, couples who could easily throw in the towel on a difficult marriage but who are determined to make it by the grace of God. For all of these, as for the disciples, God has not re-suscitated the old world, he has given birth to the new. They are living res-urrection life now.

But there's the other side of the coin—Jesus' soul-bracing promise: "I am the resurrection and the life. Those who believe in me . . . will never die" (11:25). When my dearest friend, Buford Dickinson, died, it was John Birk-beck, my Scottish Presbyterian preacher friend and spiritual mentor, who gave me this beautiful word, "For the Christian, death is not a period in the written sentence of life—but a comma—for eternal life is our gift from God through Christ."

These were not vacuous words, lacking content for John. He died one week before Easter, when he was eighty. He had been sick for a long time, often des-perately struggling to breathe because of fluid around his heart. Our letter ex-change during his last months was a great source of joy and strength for me. I miss that, but I'll carry with me forever the memory of our last three hours together.

I was in London for a meeting, and, knowing that John was not long with us, I took a plane to Aberdeen, the city where he had been a pastor and to which he returned in retirement. He couldn't get out of bed, so we spent our three hours in his upstairs bedroom. When it came time to go, I read from Ro-mans 8—Nothing can "separate us from the love of God." Then we prayed, as the taxi that was to take me to the airport sounded its horn. I was not to be rushed; I wanted to savor his presence as long as possible. I hugged him—and not even knowing what to say or what I was saying—in my discomfort, I blurted, "I'll see you, John." He lifted his hand—and it was shaking—held it high, pointed to heaven, and in a loud, rasping whisper he said, "Tomorrow!" I'm looking forward to that—tomorrow! My brother Lloyd; my friend Buford; my preacher grandfather Lewis—tomorrow!

QUESTIONS FOR REFLECTION

How does the resurrection of Jesus affect our praying? In what way can we live eternal life now? Is there a person you need to talk to about eternal life?

38

SEEK THE LORD AND LIVE

AMOS 5:21-24; PHILEMON

Amos was probably the earliest of the writing prophets. His central message is that God is righteous and just, and he acts according to his nature.

THE DAY OF THE LORD

In an empty expression of piety and religion, the people of Israel in the time of Amos longed for "the day of the Lord." But they did not know what they were longing for. Amos proclaimed that worship without justice is unacceptable to God. Unless they began practicing righteousness and justice, God's judgment was going to be harsh. "Alas for you who desire the day of the LORD," he warned. That day will be a surprise "as if someone fled from a lion, and was met by a bear" (5:18-19).

Amos pleaded with them to return to God with their whole heart. He reminded them that they had abandoned God and forsaken his covenant. They performed religious rituals at the holy shrines and bragged about how righteous they were. They lived in luxury, took bribes, and cheated the poor. It was in ignorant arrogance that they longed for the "day of the Lord." They had better get the message straight; more critical—they had better get themselves straight. Being God's people did not bring favor and privilege while they were violating God's pattern of righteousness. Superficial worship, solemn assemblies that failed to acknowledge God's presence, offerings of fatted animals as a substitute for self-giving, even songs of praise and the melody of harps, did not quicken the ears of God or soften God's heart. God wants something else. "Let justice roll down like waters, / and righteousness like an ever-flowing stream" (5:24). Apart from this, you are under judgment; "I will take you into exile," says the Lord (v. 27).

It's easy for us who are would-be prophets or those of us who tend to put more emphasis on the social implications of the gospel to be more expansive in our interpretation of Amos's scathing word. He was not calling us to give up worship and festivals celebrating God's activity in history. He was calling for what we do "inside," among ourselves as God-followers, to be matched by how we live outside the bounds of our like-minded community.

JUSTICE: GOD AT WORK

"Justice" is used most often in the Bible in reference to the needs of those who have less, measured against the obligations of those who have more. It seems that, in the main, justice has to do more with distribution than retribution. We think more of retribution, don't we? In our "justice systems" we deal primarily with retribution and punishment.

Earlier today while I was writing this, I learned that a ministry we began eighteen years ago, when I was the pastor of a church in Memphis, is flourishing. It is a ministry of reconciliation and restitution. Some of us came to believe that there was little about the way our justice system was dealing with juvenile offenders that offered any hope of change and rehabilitation. We developed a program to bring the offender together with the person or persons against whom he or she had committed a crime in a face-to-face effort at reconciliation. We trained persons to be "advocates of reconciliation," to go between the offended and the offender, believing that only when we are face-to-face with the person we have injured can we experience the implications of our crime. We added to that the dynamic of restitution. To have some degree of reconciliation, the offender would make restitution by seeking to restore or "pay back" as far as possible what had been taken from the offended.

The ministry has been effective. Many juvenile offenders are "sentenced" to participate in this program, and the justice system is convinced this is the redemptive way to deal with juvenile offenders.

While the dominant expression of justice in the Bible has to do with *distribution, retribution,* and *restitution,* reconciliation—making things right—is a part of God's call for justice to roll down like waters. Justice means not allowing wrong to go unpunished or evil to go unchecked; it means challenging the greed that brings suffering to the poor and confronting systems that keep people in the bonds of economic deprivation.

PERSUASION AND INTEGRITY

It is interesting that in the "read through the Bible in a year" plan we are following, we are also reading the tiny book of Philemon the week we are reading these chapters from Amos. Philemon is about justice, God's kind of justice; it is certainly about the mercy-flavored justice we find in Jesus.

The occasion for the letter puts justice at the forefront of our thinking. Onesimus was a slave who had run away from his owner, Philemon. He was converted through the influence of Paul and became a trusted friend and co-worker with Paul during his imprisonment in Rome. For a time Paul was tempted to keep Onesimus, but the two finally agreed that Onesimus should return to his master.

The Grace-Filled Life

Slavery was a part of the fabric of that first-century society. While we can't imagine anything as horrible as slavery, and we know the power of the gospel eventually eradicated it in England and the United States, we have to appreciate how Paul navigated that system and brought the gospel to bear on Philemon's response to his runaway—now returning—slave Onesimus.

In due time, Paul sends Onesimus back to Philemon with this letter. In it he encourages Philemon to live his faith, to take the opportunity to go beyond talking about what it means to follow Christ and actually do it. This is a rational, tough, radical call that challenges a slave owner and fellow Christian to be Christian.

In this brief teaching, the power of the gospel shines through with a rare brilliance. Rehearse the story. Philemon, a wealthy man of Colossae, hears Paul, probably on one of his business trips to Ephesus. Captured by the message, he eventually becomes a Christian, along with his son and wife. He emerges as a leader in the church that grows up in Colossae, and his house becomes one of the meeting places for the new Christian community.

What about Onesimus? His story is that of the miraculous working of Christ in the life of a person. How did he meet Paul? Had he heard him personally, in Ephesus perhaps, in the company of his master, Philemon? Or had he seen such a transformation in his master after Philemon's conversion that curiosity drove him to inquire about the source of the "new religion" that was making such a difference in Philemon's entire household? We can assume that there must have been some introduction to Christianity, and perhaps to Paul, for when Onesimus "hit bottom" as a runaway slave in Rome and the freedom for which he had risked his life did not give him the meaning he sought, he turned to Paul in Rome. (See Maxie Dunnam, *The Communicator's Commentary*, vol. 8 [Word Books, 1982], pp. 412-13.)

The compelling power of the gospel is evident, but another truth is here: *the power of persuasion and the integrity of the person who shares the gospel.* Philemon was in Paul's debt, but Paul resisted making demands. He walked a tightwire of integrity. "Though I am bold enough in Christ to command you to do your duty, yet I would rather appeal to you on the basis of love" (vv. 8-9). Paul was not insensitive to issues of justice. He even offered to repay Philemon the money Onesimus took when he ran away.

These three teachings undergird three additional truths. A relationship with Christ changes us and gives us reason for living and loving. It provides power to deal with and be triumphant over circumstance, and it enables us to forgive.

How do we balance retribution and restitution in doing justice? What role should the church play in distribution as an issue of justice? With whom do you need reconciliation? Where do you need to forgive and be forgiven?

39

THE BIG IF

2 CHRONICLES 7:7-22; PSALM 116:1-14; HEBREWS 4:14-16

When I am teaching on prayer, I usually introduce a session on intercession with this question: *What if there are some things God either cannot or will not do until and unless people pray?*

That question is shocking to most of the hearers. Their first thought is that I am challenging the sovereignty of God. My response to that is another question: *Why is it such a long leap in our minds to think that God may be as dependent upon our praying as he is upon our acting?* We don't think we are challenging God's sovereignty when we affirm that God acts through persons. Deeds of mercy, acts of reconciliation, expressions of lovingkindness, deliberate righteous activity, performance that makes for peace, cups of cold water given in the name of Jesus are seen as God's work through persons. Now, why is it such a long leap in our mind to think that God may be as dependent upon our praying as he is upon our acting?

IF MY PEOPLE

So I press the question. What if there are some things God either cannot or will not do until people pray? Even a casual review of the Bible confirms the fact that the promise of God to act in our personal lives and to act in history is often connected with a condition. Conditions are laid down that we are to meet in order for God to act effectively in our lives and in the world. The classic example of it in the Old Testament is a verse from our Scripture lesson today. "If my people who are called by name will humble themselves, pray, seek my face, and turn from their wicked ways"—those are the conditions. Then God says, "Then I will hear from heaven, and will forgive their sin and heal their land" (7:14).

The classic example from the New Testament is Jesus' great metaphor of the vine and the branches (John 15). "If you abide in me, and my words abide in you"—those are the conditions. If we meet those conditions, then, says Jesus, "Ask for whatever you wish, and it will be done for you" (v. 7).

What if there are some things God either cannot or will not do until and unless people pray? As the Spirit has pressed that question upon me, some principles of prayer have become clear and a challenge is thrust upon me.

The first principle is this: *Prayer is the continuing source of power for you and me to remain obedient in love.* Our discipleship, our dynamic for witness, moves on this center—obedience in love. How much of our fervor as Christians is dependent upon the circumstances in which we find ourselves? Yet prayer is that source of strength enabling us to rise above circumstance. A pastor in a rapidly growing suburban community may not have difficulty being enthusiastic about the church; he or she can measure the growth of it in dramatic numbers. But what happens to the pastor in a remote community with a population that is dwindling, or the pastor in the inner city where lives are being torn apart like the surrounding ruptured structures? What happens to the layperson whose witness seems to fall upon deaf ears over and over again, and for whom no response seems to come for all the effort he or she puts forth? What happens to the young couple who is left childless by a mindless accident?

What happens is determined by whether we discover prayer as the continuing source of power for us to be obedient in love. The psalmist knew this. He begins,

I love the LORD, because he has heard
  my voice and my supplications.
Because he inclined his ear to me,
  therefore I will call on him as long as I live. (116:1-2)

He confirms his obedience with a prayer of commitment.

What shall I return to the LORD
  for all his bounty to me?
I will lift up the cup of salvation
  and call on the name of the LORD,
I will pay my vows to the LORD
  in the presence of all his people. (116:12-14)

A second principle is this: *Prayer is the basic identification we have with the world and with God.* Does that sound strange? Prayer is not just the basic identification we have with God; it's the basic identification we have with the world. Christian prayer destroys our false desire either to be independent of other people or independent of God. Clarence Jordan, in his *Cotton Patch New Testament*, translates 2 Corinthians 5:19 in this fashion: "God was in Christ putting his arms around the world and hugging it to himself." That's what we do when we pray. We put our arms around another person, we put our arms around a situation, we put our arms around the church, we put our arms around the world, and we hug it to ourselves and to God. That's what intercessory prayer is about.

If it is true that prayer is the source of power that keeps us obedient in love, and that it is the basic identification we have with the world and with God, *and if there are some things God cannot or will not do until and unless people pray*, the challenge is clear: *I must become bolder in my praying.*

PRAYING WITH BOLDNESS

For a long time in my life—and ministry, in fact—I hesitated to be precise in my praying. I lacked boldness, and I prayed in a general way, hedging a bit, so that my faith would not be tested if the petition I requested was not granted. It was a clear sign of my limited faith. Too many Christians are a part of my company: we lack the confident faith to pray boldly.

I also discovered another subtle but debilitating mindset that for years limited my boldness in praying. I believe this is a common dilemma. This debilitating mindset is a false humility, a false humility that makes a great virtue of self-depreciation. Very early in my ministry, in Gulfport, Mississippi, I was uniquely blessed by having Nettie Beeson in the congregation. Because of her inspiration, encouragement, and prodding, I began to read and explore the broad expanses of prayer. Because of her, we had a strong prayer emphasis in our congregation: prayer conferences, prayer retreats, prayer groups, prayer chains. And because of Ms. Beeson's long and disciplined growth in prayer, I had the opportunity to come in touch with those whom I deem to be the giants of prayer; persons like Louise Eggleston, E. Stanley Jones, Frank Laubaugh, Estelle Carver, Tom Carruth, and others.

While I count those contacts and relationships as some of the most significant growth encounters of my life, I began to do a very stupid thing. I began to compare my prayer life to the prayer life of these persons. Measuring myself by their stature, you know where I came out—a pygmy. Thus, my false humility and my self-depreciation. For many years I found myself cowering back in prayer, thinking, who am I to pretend such boldness in prayer?

What I discovered has given me boldness. When I am authentically humble, when I see my weakness in its proper light, I can acknowledge that weakness without self-depreciation. I can glory in the weakness, knowing this is the one condition necessary to appropriate the power of Christ.

We can be bold in our praying because the secret is not in us. The writer to the Hebrews makes that abundantly clear:

> For we do not have a high priest who is unable to sympathize with our weaknesses, but we have one who in every respect has been tested as we are, yet without sin. Let us therefore approach the throne of grace with boldness, so that we may receive mercy and find grace to help in time of need. (4:15-16)

What if there are some things God either cannot or will not do until and unless people pray? If that is true, then there is another equally challenging question: *What are we going to do about it?*

QUESTIONS FOR REFLECTION

How would you describe your praying: habitual? timid? episodic? persistent? bold? How does your prayer life need to change? What are the "conditions" you need to meet for your praying to be more effective?

40

JONAH: THE RELUCTANT MISSIONARY

JONAH 4:6-11; ACTS 3:1-10

The story of Jonah is one of the most familiar in the Bible. Children love it because it is a story of sailors and ships and a large fish that swallows a man. Add to that the fact that it is a story of courage and cowardice, prejudice and repentance, the call of God and Jonah's resistance, and you have one of the most unique stories in the Bible. It is really the story of a missionary, albeit a reluctant one.

At first, Jonah resisted God, and then he rebelled and tried to run from God.

YOU CANNOT RUN FROM GOD

From the book itself, we know little about Jonah—only what is said at the outset of the book, describing his call: "The word of the LORD came to Jonah son of Amittai, saying, 'Go at once to Nineveh, that great city, and cry out against it for their wickedness has come up before me' " (vv. 1-2). The only other Old Testament reference to Jonah is in 2 Kings 14:25, where we are told that Jonah, the son of Amittai of Gath-hepher, prophesied regarding Jeroboam II, a king of Israel's northern kingdom.

Old Testament scholar Sandra Richter reminds us that

> this note places Jonah somewhere in the eight century B.C.E, and it speaks of him in relationship to both the northern and southern kingdoms of Israel. This indicates that Jonah had a well-known ministry throughout the country. The fact that he hailed from Gath-hepher, an obscure little village in the far north (see Josh. 19:13), further indicates that this man's ministry must have won him significant notoriety in his day. Yet the only story we have regarding his life and ministry is his call to Nineveh. It would seem that this must be an important story indeed. (*World Mission in the Wesleyan Spirit,* ed. Darrell L. Whiteman and Gerald H. Anderson [Providence House Publishers, 2009], pp. 28-29)

The story begins with God's call. *God does call.* We must guard against diminishing the "call" of every Christian to be a faithful disciple by always focusing on the specific call to some people like Jonah. We will come back to the story of Peter and John healing a crippled beggar, but for now register Peter's response to the beggar: "I have no silver or gold [to give you], but what I have I give you, in the name of Jesus Christ of Nazareth, stand up and walk" (Acts 3:6). No Christian is exempt from the call to minister, to use and give what he or she has in the name of Christ.

It helps to remember, at every stage of life, God's call is never simply a request; it is a command. Nor is his call a one-time event. He calls all along the way, and faithful followers have to make on-course adjustments. This is what was happening with Jonah. God was calling, but Jonah not only resisted, he sought to run away "to Tarshish from the presence of the LORD" (1:3).

Is there at least symbolic meaning in the fact that Jonah headed for Tarshish rather than to Nineveh? Nineveh was due east, and Tarshish was the most western point of the world known at that time. That's the nature of rebellion. It takes us even further away from God and what we know and love most than we intended when we initially turned away.

As I write this, my heart is heavy over a phone call I received two nights ago. It came from New York, from a woman who was active in our congregation in Memphis twenty years ago. She was in her early twenties then, a beautiful, dynamic person, but as too often happens, her casual recreational use of drugs accelerated. She married an addict. He died a few years after their marriage. From then until now, she has been engaged in a warfare with addiction. She kept crying over the phone, "If I had only known . . . if I had only known." The fact is we don't chart the course our rebellion will take us.

The next part of Jonah's story has confounded Bible readers for all the ages. Jonah boarded the ship for Tarshish, but God was in control. A great storm arose, and Jonah was cast into the sea and swallowed by a whale. All sorts of funny stories illustrate how people respond to this dramatic event. One of my favorites is of the preacher who, having preached on this story, had a critic confront him. "Preacher, how do you know it was a whale that swallowed Jonah?" The preacher said, "Well, I don't know, but when I get to heaven I'll ask Jonah." The critic responded, "But what if Jonah is not in heaven?" The preacher replied, "Then you ask him."

For me, the whale story is comparable to God delivering Israel out of Egypt or coming to us in the flesh of Jesus Christ. So I pay attention to it. It led Jonah to pray, to be delivered, and to go to where God had called him to go. And the greater miracle of the story is what happened in Nineveh—perhaps the greatest revival recorded in the Bible. Yet Jonah continues to contend with God. How strange! He is displeased and becomes angry because God kept his word and saved the city.

Though we are reflecting on Jonah, the message is not primarily about Jonah or Nineveh; it is about the character of God, the Lord of the cosmos.

> He can hurl wind. He can appoint a whale, a plant, a worm, the wind. . . . God's messengers are in his hand. If he sees the need, God will cast those messengers into the sea. But he is equally capable of rescuing them, even if that rescue

requires the most unusual lifeguard of all time . . . as the Lord of the cosmos, (he) cares about every man, woman, and child on this planet. (Richter, p. 36)

RISE UP AND WALK

And now we turn to the story of Peter and John in the book of Acts. How different in attitude, demeanor, and faithfulness from Jonah. They were on their way to the temple to pray—not contending against God and resisting his call but seeking to live it out faithfully. In the temple court they see a lame man. *They see him.* That means they were intent in their caring and compassion. Scripture says, "Peter looked intently at him, as did John, and said, 'Look at us' " (Acts 3:4). No doubt the lame man expected some money from them, but he received something else. "I have no silver or gold," Peter said, "but what I have I give you; in the name of Jesus . . . stand up and walk" (v. 6).

How unlike the reluctance of Jonah, and what lessons the story holds for us. As Christians, we are all called. We are called to care. We will not share if we don't care. We can't share what we don't have. Yet if we have experienced God's grace, it's difficult to keep it to ourselves.

QUESTIONS FOR REFLECTION

Where is God calling you to today? For what ministries is God equipping you? Who witnesses God's love to you?

41

WHAT DOES THE LORD REQUIRE OF YOU?

MICAH 6:1-8

It is printed on the wall of the Library of Congress, a Scripture verse many learned in Sunday school. Some describe it as the definition of real religion.

He has told you, O mortal, what is good;
 and what does the LORD require of you
but to do justice, and to love kindness,
 and to walk humbly with your God? (Micah 6:8)

The words are as valid today as they were twenty-eight hundred years ago when Micah wrote them.

Micah was a young contemporary of Isaiah, Hosea, and Amos in the eighth century B.C. It was a period of turmoil and change. Assyria was fast becoming a world power. The prophetic ministry of Micah and Isaiah was in Judah in the south; Hosea and Amos were in the north in Israel. There was one battle after another, with both Judah and Israel used only as pawns in the wider struggle, constantly threatened by one power or another.

There was a real kinship between Amos and Micah. Both were products of the countryside. Both proclaimed God's demand for social justice. Amos's word, "Let justice roll down like waters, / and righteousness like an ever-flowing stream" (5:24) is a parallel proclamation to Micah's call for justice, kindness, and humility.

WHAT GOD WANTS FROM US

As is not so unusual, the people didn't want to hear God's word. Micah even made a joke of that:

If someone were to go about uttering empty falsehoods,
 saying, "I will preach to you of wine and strong drink,"
 such a one would be the preacher for this people! (2:11)

Judges took bribes to render unfair judgments; priests were immoral and corrupt; prophets would prophesy anything you might want in exchange for a few shekels. Israel had grown tired of God and had chosen to go its own way. Judgment is on its way. Judah and Israel will fall.

Listen, you heads of Jacob
  and rulers of the house of Israel!
Should you not know justice?—
  you who hate the good and love the evil,
who tear the skin off my people . . .
break their bones in pieces,
  and chop them up like meat in a kettle . . .
Then they will cry to the LORD,
  but he will not answer them;
he will hide his face from them at that time,
  because they have acted wickedly. (3:1-4)

John Wesley took Micah's gritty reprimand against the corrupt leaders of Israel as an indictment against the institutional church. He took aim at unjust ministers and rulers of the church. He railed against "shepherds" who refused to rebuke gross sin for fear of losing pay or position, "those who commit abominable sins of omission 'seek themselves and not Christ crucified.' He compares them to those who strip the poor instead of clothing them" (*Wesley Study Bible*, p. 1114). We preachers and church leaders have a heavy responsibility. We are called to speak for God, not to please the people.

I have had all sorts of preaching opportunities through the years, in addition preaching to the congregations of which I have been the pastor. The occasion to which I come with the most fear and trembling is an ordination service, when young men and women are being affirmed and charged by the church for lifelong clergy leadership. I often choose Paul's charge to young Timothy (2 Tim. 4:1-5) as a text for these occasions. Paul is both pastoral and prophetic. In admonishing his protégé to be faithful in proclaiming God's message, he warns him,

> The time is coming when people will not put up with sound doctrine, but having itching ears, they will accumulate for themselves teachers to suit their own desires, and will turn away from listening to the truth and wander away to myths. (vv. 3-4)

Micah and the other prophets were scathing in their denunciation of people being "seduced into turning away, serving other gods and worshiping them" (Deut. 11:16). The temptation hasn't changed much. The ancient Israelites were attracted to gods of sex, power, and material things. So it is with us. But our primary idol is ourselves. We moderns are obsessed with self, forever making gods in our own image. If the "religious message" does not please our "itching ears," we marginalize it, or discount it altogether. So the temptation of the preacher/leader is to "soften" the message, to make it more palatable and less offensive.

Micah knew, and so must we. God is God! Israel had violated her covenant, and God demanded repentance and restoration to right relationship. With patience beyond measure, God makes his requirements known: do justice, love mercy, and walk humbly with God.

These are not the standards of the world; they are the standards of God's people. Justice makes sure that every person is treated fairly and has the opportunity to share in God's good gifts.

Micah said, *do* justice. That means it is not enough to wish for justice or to complain because it is lacking. This is a dynamic concept that calls on God's people to work for fairness and equality for all, particularly the weak and the powerless who are exploited by others. God's justice, however, is always flavored with mercy. More often than not, justice and mercy were connected in the preaching of the prophets. In a word similar to Micah's, Zechariah says, "Thus says the LORD of hosts: 'Render true judgments, show kindness and mercy to one another; do not oppress the widow, the orphan, the alien, or the poor' " (7:9-10).

Kindness, or *mercy*, is an action word, a matter of the will. It is not natural because we are basically selfish persons, so kindness/mercy requires decision. It may be costly, often requiring giving up something for ourselves.

BASIN AND TOWEL SERVICE

More often than not, my problem is not in not knowing what to do but in doing it. So we have the call, "Walk humbly with your God." It is our daily walk with God that energizes us, enabling us to do justice and love mercy. Worship and ritual in the temple were important to Israel; Micah and the prophets did not want to diminish that. However, it could not be a substitute for daily living in covenant with God. It was not the covenant; it empowered people to live the covenant.

Certainly since Jesus, we have a clearer picture of what it means to "walk humbly." The cross and the basin and towel are powerful symbols of "walking humbly." The cross—submission; the basin and towel—service. Bernard of Clairvaux said, "Learn the lesson that, if you are to do the work of a prophet, what you need is not a scepter but a hoe."

The argument that arose among the disciples in The Upper Room at the Last Supper was over which one of them was to be the greatest. Isn't it true that most of the time where there is trouble over who is the greatest, the primary trouble is over who is least? Most of us know we are not going to be the greatest, but we do not want to be the least.

The three directions for "real religion" cannot be separated. Walking humbly with God, living all of life in relation to God, will result in doing justice and loving mercy.

QUESTIONS FOR REFLECTION

Where in your community do you see the most glaring absence of justice? Where in your community do you see an inspiring commitment to justice flavored with mercy? Which of the three directions for "real religion" is most present in your life? Which is most absent?

42

God's Say-so

ACTS 7:54-60; HEBREWS 11:35-40; HEBREWS 13:1-6

Estonia was the only republic in the former Soviet Union where the Methodist Church openly survived, with a few congregations continuing to gather for worship. A great price of suffering and even death was paid for her survival. I hope I will never forget my first visit to Estonia. I met the man who personified the sacrificial faith that kept the church "open." His name was Alexander Koom. During the time of Stalin, when the church was savagely oppressed and persecuted, governmental leaders came to Brother Koom one day and told him that the Methodist Church had to be either dissolved or merged with another denomination. Brother Koom refused. The authorities told him that it would be easier for him to give in and merge the church with another, rather than having the government force the church to close. "What difference does it make," they asked, "whether you take the easy way without raising a lot of questions, or we force the issue? Whatever the case, the church is going to be banished."

Brother Koom painted a powerful picture of faith in his response. "There is all the difference in the world," he said. "If you give me a rope and tell me to hang myself, and I do so, then I am responsible; but if you hang me, you are responsible." He was sentenced to twenty-five years in Siberian exile but was miraculously released after five years. While he was in prison, the church grew even stronger because of his powerful witness—his willingness to risk even death because of his faith.

A MODERN-DAY SAINT

On my first visit there, I could just as well have been visiting with one of the New Testament churches. I knew I was among people who were a part of that line of splendor described in Hebrews 11—people of faith. I knew Brother Koom would have been as willing as Stephen to be stoned rather than to deny the faith.

I hope I will never forget that crowded church on Sunday morning. I want to carry in my mind forever the picture of those people, young and old, kneeling in prayer with tears flowing down their faces, yet smiling through the tears. I hope I will never forget their trembling hands and my trembling hand as I shared with them the bread and wine, the body and blood of our Lord Jesus Christ.

Since then, I have had a number of similar experiences; I have seen it in China, Cuba, the Czech Republic, and many of the Eastern European countries. I have seen Christians who have witnessed to Christ in the face of persecution and the threat of death.

Soon after my return from that first visit to Estonia, I was using Oswald Chamber's classic devotional book *My Utmost for His Highest*. I came to a meditation that began with this sentence from Hebrews, *"He hath said . . . so that we may boldly say . . ."* then came these two sentences, "My say-so is to be built on God's say-so. God says, 'I will never leave thee,' then I can with good courage say—'The Lord is my helper, I will not fear'" (Meditation for June 5).

Do you see the power of that? Because God has said, "I will never leave you," you and I can say, "I will not be afraid."

STANDING ON THE PROMISES

Courage and certainty don't come easy, especially in days like ours. It looks like there will be more homicides this year in my city, Memphis, than at any time during the past decade. We are getting some reports that the economic situation is getting better, but I can't find anyone who has yet experienced the turnaround. The AIDS/HIV pandemic is so threatening that we try desperately not to think about it, but it won't go away because we shut it out of our awareness. In a recent year, 50 percent of the African American men in Los Angeles, Philadelphia, and Chicago were either in jail or prison, on parole, or waiting for trial. At least 50 percent of the babies born this year will be born to unmarried mothers.

It is easy for apprehension, fear, and our own frailty to get between God's say-so and our sense of security, peace, and hope. Ironically, it is our apprehension, fear, and frailty that should turn us to God. Faith and memory must be wed. There is a guiding story in 1 Samuel to help us here. When the Israelites defeated the Philistines in a decisive battle, Samuel took a stone, placed it on that site to commemorate the victory, and named it Ebenezer. He said, "Thus far the LORD has helped us" (7:12). Most of us can muster the memory of being helped by God. That memory enables us to claim faith in the present more readily. But even if we have difficulty retrieving such a memory, we must trust God's promise. The witness of millions through the ages verifies that trust.

In Moses' encounter with God at the burning bush, God named himself "I am." Think about it. God didn't say his name is "I was" or "I will be." Helen Mallicoat wrote a poem about this—hearing God say, "Do not live in the past for I am not there . . . / Do not live in the future for I am not there." God is "I am," and wants to meet us in the present moment. That is God's ultimate Say-so. We can claim his promise now, this very moment, and always. We will never be where God is not, and we will never have a need that God cannot meet or cannot give us the resources to live without that need being met.

REAL STRANGERS AND REAL FRIENDS

In this Hebrews passage there is another challenge: "Do not neglect to show hospitality to strangers, for by doing that some have entertained angels without knowing it" (13:2). It's a simple, lucent picture of a primary mark of a Christian: *hospitality*.

The sign of God's people is always a welcome sign. *The welcome mat must always lie at the door of the Christian's heart.*

I doubt if the author of Hebrews was talking about the masses of anonymous humanity that pass us by in the shopping center or on a downtown busy street. More likely, he was talking about those people we encounter on our jobs, in our schools, at social functions, even in church. So many of these are the "real strangers" among us. We may know a good bit about the outer expressions of their lives, but how much do we know about what's going on inside?

Peter Walker was a teenager who took his own life. Everyone who heard was shocked that this bright, cheerful person who came from such a caring family and whose life held such promise would kill himself. After his death, Peter's journal was found hidden under his bed. In it he wrote of how isolated he felt,

I missed your love and warmth within,
But most of all, whoever you are, I missed you.
—Brenda Rabkin, *Growing Up Dead* (Abingdon, 1978), p. 118

There are people like Peter all around us. We don't know who they are, but be sure of this: if we practice hospitality and allow our hearts to be open doors of attention and care, they will emerge. Hopefully they will find the open door of hospitality before they handle their pain, isolation, and despair as Peter did. In his book *The Weight of Glory*, C. S. Lewis made this bold claim, "Next to the sacraments themselves, your neighbor is the holiest object presented to your senses." Our neighbor may be that stranger to whom we are called to show hospitality.

QUESTIONS FOR REFLECTION

Spend some time reflecting on experiences in your life that confirm God's promise, "I will never leave you nor forsake you." As you look back on your life, what have been the occasions of greatest fear? What were the sources of those fears? Did you seek the presence of God? Do you know your neighbors where you live? How can you enrich and deepen the friendships you already have?

43

"But If Not" Faith

HABAKKUK 3:17-19; PSALM 124

The prophet Habakkuk is one of the "minor" prophets. He is probably best-known for one line: "The righteous live by their faith" (2:4). That is the source of Paul's famous phrase found in his Letter to the Romans, particularly, "The just shall live by faith" (Rom. 1:17). Paul used this affirmation to construct his argument about justification by grace through faith in Romans and Galatians. It later became a battle cry for the Reformation.

In the passage where this wonderful phrase appears, the prophet says,

> I will stand at my watchpost . . .
> to see what he will say to me. . . .
> Write the vision;
>   make it plain on tablets,
>   so that a runner may read it.
> For there is still a vision. . . .
> If it seems to tarry, wait for it;
>   it will surely come. (2:1-3)

Like other prophets, Habakkuk sees himself standing on a wall, speaking to and waiting for a word from the Lord.

THE LORD IS MY STRENGTH

In dialogue with God, Habakkuk struggles with the question with which most of us wrestle at one time or another: Why does the Lord permit the righteous to suffer while the wicked prosper? He concludes that those who trust in their own power and might will ultimately experience defeat, but "the righteous live by faith."

Alexander MacLaren refers to Habakkuk as "one of the most magnificent pieces of imaginative poetry in Scripture or anywhere else" (*Exposition of Holy Scripture*, Vol. 6 [Grand Rapids: Baker Books, 1982], p. 238). Having described the great delivering manifestation of the Most High God, the one who "shed awe and terror over his soul" (MacLaren, p. 238). Habakkuk vows that in this God of his salvation he will rejoice, no matter what privation and suffering he may undergo. He concludes with a description of who and what God can be for those who put their trust and gladness in him. That description comes as a finale in verses 17-19, concluding,

GOD, the Lord, is my strength;
  he makes my feet like the feet of a deer,
  and makes me tread upon the heights.

This affirmation is almost verbatim of a part of the eighteenth psalm.

For who is God except the LORD? . . .
He made my feet like the feet of a deer,
  and set me secure on the heights (vv. 31, 33)

In both instances, it is an expression of joy in response to the manifestation of the delivering power of God.

This concluding prayer of Habakkuk is in the company of the prayer of Shadrach, Meshach, and Abednego. They were caught between Nebuchadnezzar and the fiery furnace. They might have said, "This is the bitter, unjust, hopeless end." But they didn't. They shocked King Nebuchadnezzar, denying him to his face, as they swept the despair from their souls and declared, "Our God can and will deliver us," *but if not* . . . Those three words shatter the might of Babylon. "But if not [if we are not delivered] . . . we will not serve your gods" (see Dan. 3:16).

FAITH TO MOVE MOUNTAINS AND BRING DOWN WALLS

I am intrigued by the fact that if you are following our "read through the Bible in a year" plan, Psalm 124 comes the week we are reading Habakkuk. In an upcoming devotion (No. 49), I tell the story of participating in conferring the World Methodist Peace Award to Pastor Beslov Zdrovko of Bulgaria. Our bestowing that award was an unforgettable celebration of his courageous, persistent, and ardent commitment to the Christian faith—a "but if not" faith for which people willingly risked their lives, indeed, for which many died. It was that faith that eventually brought down the Berlin Wall and the crumbling of the Soviet Union. At our celebration, a layperson, Bedros Altoonian, read Psalm 124. He said it was the psalm of the Bulgarian Church. We understood why, given their years of suffering.

If it had not been the LORD who was on our side . . .
  when our enemies attacked us,
then they would have swallowed us up alive . . .
then the flood would have swept us away. . . .
Blessed be the LORD,
  who has not given us
  as prey to their teeth.
We have escaped like a bird
  from the snare of the fowlers. . . .
Our help is in the name of the LORD.

Here is a part of that "but if not" faith story. Early in the Communist regime, when churches were being taken over or destroyed, the Methodist Church in the center of Varna was destroyed. The bell tower was pushed down. In the middle of the night, two young men took the bell out of the destroyed tower and buried it in the backyard of one of these young men.

When we were there in 1991 to confer the Peace Award, we broke ground to rebuild that church. Building proceeded slowly, as money was available. After three years in the process, the building project was closed down. This was a political action for which there was no explanation. There was no building activity downtown for nearly four years.

But the church was finally completed, and on Sunday, September 29, 2002, there was an official dedication. The Superintendent of the Church of Bulgaria presided at the dedication. His name was Bedros Altoonian. Remember? He was the layperson who read the Bulgarian Methodist Psalm back in 1991. Soon after our time there in 1991, since there were only three pastors left after the ravages of Communism, the Bishop of that central conference of the Methodist Church ordained Altoonian as a pastor. He was so effective that he soon became the Superintendent of all the work.

Now the rest of the story. Bedros Altoonian was one of the two young men who had rescued the bell from the destroyed tower more than twenty years before and had buried it in his backyard. That bell was now a part of the church in the city center of Varna, and it was officially rung for the first time on September 29, 2002.

The Bulgarian Methodists have their Psalm, and they verify the faith of Habakkuk.

Though the fig tree does not blossom,
   and no fruit is on the vines . . .
yet I will rejoice in the LORD;
   I will exult in the God of my salvation.
GOD, the Lord is my strength. (3:17-19)

QUESTIONS FOR REFLECTION

Have you ever been put in an uncomfortable situation because of your faith? What in your experience gives clearest witness to God's presence and deliverance? In what ways are you demonstrating your confidence that "GOD, the Lord is my strength"?

44

GOD'S CHOSEN PEOPLE

DEUTERONOMY 6:4-9; DEUTERONOMY 7:1-10; ZEPHANIAH 3:17-20

It is impossible to read the Old Testament without dealing with the con-cept of covenant. God chose Israel to be his chosen people. He made a covenant (agreement) with them at Mount Sinai. "I . . . will be your God, and you shall be my people" (Lev. 26:12) sums it up.

YOU ARE CHOSEN BY GOD

The New Testament is "the new covenant" in Christ Jesus. Again, "chosen people" is a prominent designation. We see it clearly in 1 Peter 2:9-10:

> You are a chosen race, a royal priesthood, a holy nation, God's own people, in order that you may proclaim the mighty acts of him who called you out of dark-ness into his marvelous light:
> Once you were not a people,
>   but now you are God's people;
> once you had not received mercy,
>   but now you have received mercy.

It is easy to see that this passage is rooted in the Old Testament concept of the covenant. The people of God were those people with whom God had made a covenant. Verse 10 of 1 Peter can be seen as a fulfillment of Hosea's render-ing of God's promise in Hosea 2:23:

> I will have mercy upon her who had not obtained mercy;
> Then I will say to those who were not My people,
> "You are My people!"
> And they shall say "You are my God!" (NKJV).

Note that Peter is quoting Hosea almost verbatim, and the descriptive titles he applies to the church, the "new Israel," are all titles prominent in the Old Testament as designations for God's people: "a chosen race, a royal priesthood, a holy nation, God's own people." The phrase translated "God's own people" literally means "a people of God's possession." The King James Version trans-lates it "a peculiar people."

A dictionary definition of *peculiar* says: "out of the ordinary, strange, odd, unusual," and that's the way we normally use the word. We refer to persons we think a bit odd or weird as peculiar. But the word has a far more expansive meaning than that. It means "special" or "one of a kind." It comes from the Latin, and among its original meanings was "a slave is private property." As Christians our relationship to God is unique; we are God's people, God's possession. We remember how God referred to Israel, "the people whom I formed for myself / so that they might declare my praise" (Isa. 43:21). Then there is this sad word about Israel, "You were unmindful of the Rock that bore you; / you forgot the God who gave you birth" (Deut. 32:18).

In most Bibles the first part of chapter seven of Deuteronomy is titled "A Chosen People." In this section there is this eloquent description of Israel: "For you are a people holy to the LORD your God; the LORD your God has chosen you out of all the peoples on earth to be his people, his treasured possession" (7:6).

The question always is *What does it mean to be God's chosen people?* Scripture makes it clear. It was not because there was a great population of these people or because they were uniquely powerful and influential. They were really a "no people." It was because the Lord loved them that he chose them. This is what Israel was to remember, and this was the way they were to respond. "Hear, O Israel: The LORD our God, the LORD is one! You shall love the LORD your God with all your heart, with all your soul, and with all your might" (Deut. 6:4-5 NKJV). In the Jewish tradition this is known as the Shema, which is the first word in Hebrew of this imperative command: "Hear." Since at least the second century B.C., this has been the cornerstone of every Jew's confessional faithfulness. Faithful Jews recite it every morning and evening as they were commanded in Deuteronomy to do.

When Jesus was asked in Mark's Gospel which was the greatest commandment, he begins by reciting the Shema. This is the first commandment, Jesus said; then he added, "The second is this, 'You shall love your neighbor as yourself'" (12:31). The second half of Jesus' answer is intimately related to the first. In fact, Jesus combines the Shema with another charge to God's chosen people: "Love your neighbor as yourself" (Lev. 19:18).

REMEMBER WHO YOU ARE

There are two great lessons here. One, *it is crucial that we remember who we are*. Moses would not be with the Israelites to lead them into the Promised Land. Who remind them constantly that they are God's covenant people who were to worship and trust in God alone? So they were instructed to *remember who they were*.

Put these words on the doorposts of your homes. Put them on the gates of your city. Wear them on your arms and as headbands when you pray. Recite them in every worship service. Teach them to your children. Don't give in to the temptation to worship the pagan gods of the Canaanites. Remember to put God first, to worship him alone. Don't forget—he is always with you.

HEAR! When you face an uncertain future, remember—remember who you are!

HEAR! When you are tempted to idolatry, to "make a golden calf" by giving something other than God first place in your life—remember who you are!

Remember who you are. How long has it been since you were awestricken by the thought, I am chosen—chosen by God. Think about it. Think about it, and tremble.

REMEMBER GOD

The second lesson is to remember God. Our reading from Zephaniah is a guide.

REMEMBER: God is with us always. "The LORD, your God, is in your midst" (Zeph. 3:17).

REMEMBER: God will strengthen us in love. "He will rejoice over you with gladness, / he will renew you in his love" (Zeph. 3:17).

REMEMBER: God will protect and heal. "I will remove disaster from you / . . . save the lame and gather the outcast" (Zeph. 3:18-19).

REMEMBER: God will be with us even in death. "I will bring you home" (Zeph. 3:20).

Moses never made it to the Promised Land. Can you imagine how it must have felt for Moses to be so near but yet so far? He wanted so desperately to lead the people into the land he had dreamed of from the moment he responded to God's call to lead God's people out of Egypt. I can't help but believe that his comfort came as he remembered God's faithfulness. He may very well have thought what Zephaniah wrote long after: "At that time I will bring you home." Home for Moses, as for us, is the Promised Land. We sing about it even now.

> All o'er all those wide extended plains
> Shines one eternal day,
> There God, the Son, forever reigns,
> And scatters night away.
>
> When shall I reach that happy place,
> And be forever blest?
> When shall I see my Father's face,
> And in His bosom rest?

I am bound for the Promised Land,
I am bound for the Promised Land;
O who will come and go with me?
I am bound for the Promised Land.
(Samuel Stennett, 1787)

QUESTIONS FOR REFLECTION

When was the last time you were awesticken by the thought, "I am chosen by God"? What does that mean to you? In what way does the congregation of which you are a part act as "God's own people"? How does the fact that as a Christian you are "bound for the promised land" affect your daily living?

45

"O GIVE ME THAT BOOK!"

1 PETER 1:22-25; PSALM 130

John Wesley, the founder of the Methodist Movement, called himself "a man of one book." He wanted Methodists to be Bible people.

Wesley's emphasis on the primacy of scripture was based on the conviction that the Bible is "able to instruct you for salvation through faith in Christ Jesus" (2 Tim 3:15 RSV). Wesley was a person of one book because he knew the Bible was *more than a book*. It was as Paul designated it: "All Scripture is God-breathed, and is useful for teaching, rebuking, correcting and training in righteousness, so that the man of God may be thoroughly equipped for every good work" (2 Tim. 3:16-17 NIV). As for Wesley and for Christians through the ages, the Bible should be for us our primary rule of life.

Psalm 119 is a long, colorful, incisive expression of "the glories of God's law." Verse 105 is one of the best-known in the Bible: "Your word is a lamp to my feet / and a light to my path." Verses 169-76 form a kind of finale of this celebration of God's word in expressions like these: "My lips will pour forth praise, / because you teach me your statutes" (v. 171). "I long for your salvation, O LORD, / and your law is my delight" (v. 174). "Let me live that I may praise you, / and let your ordinances help me" (v. 175).

Paul counseled the Colossians to "Let the word of Christ dwell in you richly; teach and admonish one another in all wisdom; and with gratitude in your hearts sing psalms, hymns, and spiritual songs to God" (Col. 3:16).

One of the most beautiful affirmations of the meaning and power of Scripture comes from Peter. He says we "have been born anew . . . through the living and enduring word of God" (1 Peter 1:23), and then concludes,

> All flesh is like grass
> and all its glory like the flower of grass.
> The grass withers,
> and the flower falls,
> but the word of the Lord endures forever. (vv. 24-25)

HEAR THE GOOD NEWS

He then reminds his friends, "That word is the good news that was announced to you" (1 Peter 1:25). There was certainly "good news" before Peter's preaching. Psalm 130 reflects that. The psalmist knew that the good news is *that we can pray with hope*. It is this conviction that enables the psalmist to pray, "Out of the depths I cry to you. . . . / Lord, hear my voice!" (vv. 1-2). He knew that the good news is *God cares and will respond out of love.* "If you, O LORD, should mark iniquities, / Lord, who could stand? / But there is forgiveness with you, / so that you may be revered" (vv. 3-4). The psalmist knew that the good news is *God is powerful to save.* "For with the LORD there is steadfast love, / and with him is great power to redeem" (v. 7).

Peter had a more concrete expression of the good news known by the psalmist. After his initial greeting in his Letter, he sings, "Blessed be the God and Father of our Lord Jesus Christ! By his great mercy he has given us a new birth into a living hope through the resurrection of Jesus Christ from the dead" (v. 3). That's what we need, isn't it?

Few people in our day are not concerned about the current economic situation. Some are deeply worried. They are all around us. A young couple, who were seduced by the too-easy offer of a sub-prime or interest-only loan, are now losing their home. A retired couple who thought they were secure in having a regular income at age sixty-five have learned that their retirement account has been gutted, and they are losing confidence about their future. This is not restricted to economic concerns. We know persons in hospitals and nursing homes who need desperately to hear that healing, life-giving word: "born again to a living hope."

Don't we all stand on common ground? How long, O Lord, are these wars going to continue in Iraq and Afghanistan? How many more of our own military sons and daughters, how many more of the thousands of innocent persons in those sad lands are going to die before peace comes? Is there hope?

We've lived with it so long, Lord: a son, a daughter, a husband, a wife— caught in the tenacious web of addiction; a son or daughter lost in the far country of sin and destructive separation from all that would give their life meaning and make them whole. Is there hope?

The diagnosis is clear, and the doctor is honest. Apart from a miracle beyond the realm of medicine, at best our loved one may have a year to live. How do we exercise hope in the face of such devastating loss?

Into our lives and situations of desperation and despair, or the temptation to despair, into the energy-draining struggle to sense some sign of hope comes this bracing, exhilarating word from Peter: "born anew to a living hope through the resurrection of Jesus Christ from the dead" (1:3 RSV).

We can count on it. It's in the book: the Word that brings hope by pointing to our Deliverer, Jesus Christ. The Word that assures us that we have the guarantee of help—for our questions, our pains, and our wounds—in Jesus Christ. The Word that gives us confidence to draw near to the throne of grace, that we may receive mercy and find grace to help in time of need (Heb. 4:16).

The Word that brings life in the presence of death. "Truly, truly, I say to you, whoever believes has eternal life" (John 6:47 ESV).

If we open this book daily and prayerfully read and reflect, we will be amazed at the power of God's breathed word. We will understand why Wesley cried, "O give me that book!"

QUESTIONS FOR REFLECTION

How does God use the Bible to nourish your soul? What is your most recent "new learning" from Scripture? Take a few moments and memorize one of the Bible verses used in this devotion.

46

BEAUTIFUL PEOPLE NEED GOD

ACTS 16:11-15; ACTS 16:16-40

The world is full of what we usually call *beautiful people*. It's a term we use to designate those who have a special place in society, who may have been "born with a silver spoon in their mouth." They are the glamorous ones who are featured on *Lifestyles of the Rich and Famous*. We've come to refer to a whole group—actors, the rich, the jet set, the "café" society, the international set—as the "beautiful people."

If such a designation had been used in New Testament times, Lydia would have been among the beautiful people. Ellsworth Kalas calls her the "sophisticated lady" of the New Testament. See her in her setting.

For years after our Lord's death and resurrection, preaching the gospel was restricted pretty much to Asia Minor and probably the northern sections of Africa. Paul, the great missionary, changed all that. One night as he was preparing to begin another missionary journey, he had a vision. He saw and heard a man pleading, "Come over to Macedonia and help us" (Acts 16:9). Not one to disregard the call of God, Paul responded and headed across the sea to that continent. His first stop was Philippi, a major city of first-century Europe.

On the Sabbath, seeking a place of prayer, Paul and his companions went to the riverside, and there a group of women gathered around to listen to what Paul had to say. Apparently Lydia was in that group. She was a very successful woman, "a seller of purple"—purple fabrics that were a costly commodity.

Lydia is one of those persons we might call "bit actors" in Christian history. They appear only briefly, here and there on the pages of the Bible. Though we get a fleeting glimpse of them, what they teach us may be profound and challenging. This is the way God does things, isn't it? God finds someone we would not have chosen, and works in a way we would have never guessed.

WE CANNOT GO WHERE GOD IS NOT

Notice one of the very first lines describing Lydia: "A certain woman named Lydia, a worshiper of God" (16:14). It's true, isn't it? *We can't go where God is not*. Language like "we must take Christ to Afghanistan" or "we must take Christ to the prison" fails to claim an important truth. We can't go where God is not.

Several years ago I heard an unforgettable story about a mother who brought her baby to a religious temple somewhere in India. With her baby in her arms she knelt before a religious idol. Standing nearby was a Christian missionary. As she lifted her baby before the idol, the missionary could see it was sickly and deformed. Then he heard her pray: "Make my child comely and fair and whole like other children."

Later, outside the temple, the missionary approached this mother and asked her, "To whom did you pray?"

"I do not know," she answered, "but surely there is someone somewhere to hear a mother's cry and keep her heart from breaking."

Missionaries tell stories of that sort over and over again, as they witness to the fact that no matter where they go, God has stamped his image on the life of every human being. God's spirit stirs.

Thrilling stories continue coming out of Russia and the former Soviet Union. People who have been trained in atheism, their minds bombarded with a godless ideology from the time they were three years old—now when they hear a witness, or read the Bible, or attend worship, something strikes fire. They identify a burning that was in their soul all along.

Paul wrote to Timothy that it is God who wants "all men to be saved and come to a knowledge of the truth" (1 Tim. 2:4 NIV). There are monumental lessons here for the church and for our faithfulness to mission and evangelism. Let me simply name three of those lessons.

One, Christians ought not to boast about their relationship to God. One of the problems with witnessing in other cultures is that we run the risk of being arrogant about our relationship to God because we have been given the gift of Jesus Christ. Two, Christians should remain trustful and optimistic regarding the salvation of unbelievers. Three, Christians must persevere in preaching the gospel. The church is going to be challenged by this perhaps more than ever before in the years ahead. There are millions and millions of people who have not yet heard the gospel of Jesus Christ. And there are millions of people in places that have become religious lands, such as "Muslim nations," where to preach the gospel is a sacrifice, where to preach the gospel is to be under the threat of death. We must persevere in preaching the gospel. It is not our business to determine the result of that preaching—we share the good news of Jesus Christ with everyone, and we leave to God the business of harvesting.

MINISTRY BELONGS TO EVERYONE

So the first lesson Lydia teaches us is that we cannot go where God is not. A second lesson that Lydia teaches us is that ministry belongs to everyone. Women in ordained ministry is a big issue in our day. A number of denominations are divided over the question of ordaining women. I'm happy that

The Grace-Filled Life

Methodism has been ordaining women for over a hundred years. More than that, I'm happy that women have provided leadership in ministry throughout the history of Christianity. The first witnesses to the resurrection of Jesus were women. And Lydia is a great witness to the fact that ministry belongs to everyone. Not just ordained ministers, men or women, but every baptized Christian is a minister.

Now, close to these two truths is another one: the Gospel has the power to reach people wherever they are. It's interesting that the story of Lydia is in the same chapter of Acts as that of the Philippian jailer. Paul and Silas were in prison, but where they were was not an issue. They sang and prayed, an earthquake came, prisoners' chains were unfastened, the doors of the prison opened, and the jailer was flabbergasted. Thinking all the prisoners were going to escape and he would be held responsible, he drew his sword and was about to kill himself when Paul intervened: "Don't harm yourself! We are all here" (Acts 16:28 NIV). The jailer was overcome with the Spirit of God, fell down at the feet of Paul and Silas and said, "Sirs, what must I do to be saved?" (v. 30). The rest of the story is that he believed in Christ, and he and his entire household were baptized. The gospel has the power to reach and save people wherever they are.

When I was a pastor in Memphis, my wife, Jerry, and a number of people in our church provided a ministry for the women at the county jail. Pastors would go into the jail on Thursday evening to preach and pray with the prisoners. Women in our church served in all sorts of ways, and amazing things came out of that experience. Here is one of those stories Jerry recorded in her journal.

After preaching and the Eucharist . . . the women were asked to give a testimony. A young woman came forward. She leaned on the side of the pulpit . . . wringing her hands and began to cry. With emotions stirring deep within, she told her story. She said this was her first arrest . . . her first time in jail and that she was not guilty. In her words she said, "I was taking a shower at my mama's house when the police came looking for my mama. At first they thought I was my mama. My mama was not at home so they arrested me for drugs found in the house. I don't do drugs! My mama should be here. . . . I'm not guilty. . . . I'm doing my mama's time! I'm doing my mama's time!"

Then Jerry prayed . . .

Lord . . . tonight my ears were opened to see! As the young woman wept over and over, "I'm not guilty . . . I'm not guilty . . . I'm doing my mama's time!" I thought of what you did for me! You were not guilty yet you did my time. You too agonized and longed for another way, yet you were obedient to our Father's will. Though not guilty of my sins, you did my time.

Because Christ did our time and died for us, the gospel has the power to reach people wherever they are.

QUESTIONS FOR REFLECTION

Have you been anywhere lately and surprisingly found God there as well? How are you living out the claim that ministry belongs to everyone? How do you and your congregation share in making sure the gospel is preached everywhere?

47

HELP WHEN WE NEED IT

ACTS 18:1-11; PSALM 136:23-24

Athens, Greece was the center of great learning, a kind of hotbed for many religious expressions. There were "gods" of all sorts, and temples in which to worship them.

Leading intellectuals of Athens invited Paul to share more about the "new" faith he was espousing. He began by addressing these persons where they were.

> Athenians, I see how extremely religious you are in every way. For as I went through the city and looked carefully at the objects of your worship, I found among them an altar with the inscription, "To an unknown god." What therefore you worship as unknown, this I proclaim to you. (Acts 17:22-23)

THE UNKNOWN GOD

Paul went on to make his case for the God who had come to us in Jesus Christ, having as the centerpiece of his argument the affirmation, "In him we live and move and have our being" (Acts 17:28). It was a brilliant presentation of the gospel. Yet, as clear and as powerful as it was, the intellectuals of Athens were not convinced.

From Athens Paul went to Corinth. You get a clear picture of what Paul experienced in Corinth from the first five verses of the second chapter of 1 Corinthians:

> When I came to you, brothers and sisters, I did not come proclaiming the mystery of God to you in lofty words or wisdom. For I decided to know nothing among you except Jesus Christ, and him crucified. And I came to you in weakness and in fear and in much trembling. My speech and my proclamation were not with plausible words of wisdom, but with a demonstration of the Spirit and of power, so that your faith might rest not on human wisdom but on the power of God.

Do you feel the depth of humility as well as the discouragement Paul was feeling? Further discouragement awaited him there in Corinth. He had been driven out of Macedonia, and barely tolerated in Athens, and now in Corinth he met the same hostility he had experienced before. The lessons we learn from his experience in Corinth are about more than apologetics—how we share the gospel—it is about how we remain faithful when living and sharing the gospel is difficult.

None of us is immune to disappointment, fear, or failure. It will help us to look at Paul, who said he came to Corinth in weakness and in much fear and trembling. The Lord did two things to give Paul strength and courage.

First, *he gave him the gift of new friends*. Aquila and Priscilla became great supporters of Paul. Then Silas and Timothy came from Macedonia. What a difference these friends made. I don't believe it is accidental that Luke recorded what happened in this fashion. It was when Paul had the support of his friends that he was compelled to testify.

We can count on it. God will give us those friends we need to share the gospel mission with others. A dimension of that is also our need to be attentive to God, who might want us to be the friend someone needs for ongoing Kingdom work.

The second thing God did for Paul was *give him a new vision*. He came to him in a vision one night, telling him not to be afraid, to speak and not be silent, "for I am with you, and no one will lay a hand on you to harm you, for there are many in this city who are my people" (vv. 9-10). That's the way the Lord works: if we trust him, he will come at the time when we need him to give us a new vision and hope.

Added to this new vision was a perfectly timed specific intervention from an unlikely source. The Lord seldom works apart from persons. The person was Gallio. He refused to respond to the accusations of the Jews against Paul, and he dismissed their public case against him.

Gallio did not know that he was the Lord's instrument of intervention, but that's the serendipitous way the Lord works. It was that decision of Gallio that made it possible for Paul to remain in Corinth "a considerable time"—long enough to finish his work. His time in Corinth was one of the most strategic in his ministry. In Corinth, he taught, established one of the great New Testament churches, wrote the Thessalonian Epistles, and was reconfirmed in his call and relationship to the Lord. His time of discouragement and disappointment was over, and he left in the freedom and power the Spirit provides. Again, he might have been remembering some Scripture, perhaps Psalm 136, where the writer rehearsed the mighty acts of God in history, concluding with the affirmation

It is he who remembered us in our low estate,
　for his steadfast love endures forever;
and rescued us from our foes,
　for his steadfast love endures forever. (v. 23-24)

When and where have you had the most difficulty sharing your faith? Who are the friends who have been sent to you from God? Who can you be a "God-send" for today?

48

Coram Deo

MALACHI 4:1-5; PSALM 139:1-13, 23-24

The fact of judgment is prominent in Scripture. There is no way to edit out the fact that both persons and nations stand in judgment before God. God's judgment is an essential part of the biblical understanding of life.

In the last book of the Old Testament, the prophet Malachi described what he thought the Day of Judgment would be like. "The day is coming, burning like an oven, when all the arrogant and all evildoers will be stubble; the day that comes shall burn them up, says the LORD of hosts, so that it will leave them neither root nor branch" (4:1).

Book after book in the Bible sounds a similar note: there will be a Day of Judgment. It is interesting that the last book of the Old Testament has this note of judgment in the last chapter, and the first book in the New Testament, Matthew, is sometimes called *The Gospel of Judgment.*

> More than all the other Gospels, it deals with the notion of divine judgment in history and a day of judgment at the end of history. Matthew devotes two full chapters (24–25) to Jesus' words about divine judgment and to his stern warning to the disciples to be ready for the day of tribulation, for the day of reckoning when the master returns, for the appearance of the Son of Man. (Maxie Dunnam, *Twelve Parables of Jesus* [Cokesbury, 1988], p. 12)

Chapter 24 of Matthew includes Jesus foretelling the destruction of the Temple because of the disobedience of Israel and a vivid picture of the days immediately before the Day of Judgment when the Son of Man will come to judge the world. Then in chapter 25, there are three very familiar parables about judgment and about being prepared at all times. The most famous of these gives the basis of how we will be judged: "Inasmuch as you did it unto the least of these, you did it to me," or "Inasmuch as you did not do it to the least of these, you did not do it to Me" (v. 45, KJV).

IN THE MEANTIME

The lesson is clear. God is good and demands of us a life of righteousness. God is not neutral; sin is serious to God. This does not mean that we are to live in fear; nor does it mean that God is primarily an angry sovereign, holding persons by a spider web over a raging pit of fire. It means we live with the eyes of our hearts open, aware that to live is to choose. One day judgment will come, so what do we do in the meantime?

I believe Psalm 139 is a helpful guide. The psalmist's prayer reflects on God's constant presence in every stage of life, in every circumstance. With penetrating insight and probing discernment, the psalmist paints an honest, revealing picture of who we are in relation to God.

God knows me (vv. 1-6). He knows perfectly all my weakness and all my strength, all my thoughts and all my fears, all my secret desires and all my holy aspirations, all my needs and all my deepest yearnings. We can delight in this. "Such knowledge is too wonderful for me" (v. 6).

God is with me (vv. 7-10). For the psalmist, as with us when we fully realize it, it was a startling revelation that he cannot get away from God. It's a thrilling thought, though a sobering one: God is always near. This is a personal matter, and what could be more heartening? "Where can I go from your spirit? / Or where can I flee from your presence?"(v. 7). Not only is it heartening but also sobering and challenging as it relates to judgment. We will come back to this in a moment.

God formed me (vv. 13-18). God is our creator. That means we are precious to him, and he has the right to have expectations of us and to make demands of us. Though not to the degree of our awareness, the psalmist knew that not only had God formed him but that he would complete him: "I come to the end—I am still with you" (v. 18). We know we were formed, but we also know we were ransomed by this God of love through his Son, Jesus.

The last verses of the psalm are a prescription for how we are to live, waiting for the judgment.

> Search me, O God, and know my heart;
>   test me and know my thoughts.
> See if there is any wicked way in me,
>   and lead me in the way everlasting. (vv. 23-24)

JUDGMENT AND GRACE

We cannot, even if we wish, live in the dark away from God. We live self-consciously—that is intentionally—in openness to God. *Coram Deo* is a Latin phrase that captures it best. Translated it means "in the presence of God" and summarizes the idea of Christians living in the presence of, under the authority of, and to the honor and glory of God. Whatever we do and wherever we do it, we are acting in the present and under the gaze of God.

In the view of the psalmist, and more fully in the Christian view of reality, this means both judgment and grace.

QUESTIONS FOR REFLECTION

How does the fact of judgment influence the way you live? Where do you need to ask God for help to eliminate sin in your life? What changes do you need so that you will have an increased awareness of the presence of God?

49

HEAR WHAT THE SPIRIT IS SAYING

REVELATION 3:7-13; 1 JOHN 5:1-5

> *"The Revelation was not written without tears; neither without tears will it be understood" (Notes, Rev. 5:4). With these words, Wesley puts readers on notice that if they intend to join with John in experiencing God's revelation, they must be prepared to do so fully, with emotions as well as intellect. These "words of the prophecy" (1:3) draw upon all our senses to see, hear, touch, smell, even taste the word of God for today. Perhaps this is one reason why the book has been so hard to resist for poets, painters, musicians, and a variety of other artists, who are often among its best interpreters.* (Wesley Study Bible, p. 1537)

With that introductory word to the Book of Revelation by the editors of the *Wesley Study Bible,* I share a Revelation experience centered on our specific reading from the book.

TASTE THE WORD OF GOD FOR TODAY

I hope I will never forget my visit to Bulgaria in September 1991. The Executive Committee of the World Methodist Council was meeting there because we were honoring the Superintendent of the tiny Methodist Church of Bulgaria with the World Methodist Peace Award. This award has been given to people whose names are known all over the world: Jimmy Carter, Anwar Sadat, Mikhail Gorbachev, Desmond Tutu, and other well-known persons. But now it was being given to a simple Methodist preacher, Zdravko Beslov. The choice of the honoree was right because of his role his church had played in the collapse of a godless atheistic system.

On Sunday, following the Peace Award ceremony on Friday, Pastor Beslov preached in a worship service in the mother church of Methodism in Bulgaria, in the capital city, Sofia. Preaching has been defined as truth communicated through personality. I experienced that kind of preaching, but I also experienced *Revelation* "with tears"—more with my emotion than with my intellect.

Pastor Beslov's text was Revelation 3:7-12. This passage comes from a series of messages the angel of the Lord delivered to the seven churches in Asia Minor. This particular word was for the church in Philadelphia. I knew we were in for a significant encounter with God's word when he began to read, "Let anyone who has an ear listen to what the Spirit is saying to the churches. . . . These are the words of the holy one, the true one, / who has the key of David, / who opens and no one will shut, / who shuts and no one opens" (vv. 6-7).

Talk about the Word becoming flesh: there it was in the midst of us. The few Christians in that land had little power. Many of them had been put to death for their faith. Pastor Beslov had been in prison for sixteen years, a number of those years in a cave that had been turned into a jail. His body was racked with painful arthritis, and he could hardly walk because of that experience. "I know that you have but little power, and yet you have kept my word and have not denied my name" (v. 8).

Then there was verse 9: "I will make those of the synagogue of Satan . . . come and bow down before your feet, and they will learn that I have loved you." An entire government system had opposed the church. A godless system had imprisoned those who even hinted at the fact that they might believe in God. But now the system was collapsing, and people were learning that Christ had loved these faithful people, and had loved them with an undying love that enabled them to survive the worst of oppression.

Pastor Beslov witnessed in his life and in his words to the power of God's word—alive in a contemporary way. There was no sign of power in the Christian community for over forty years in the way the secular system was defining and using power. Christians were driven underground, and they met in hiding. Many of them had to practice their faith in secret. They knew the promise of the Revelation: "Because you have kept my word of patient endurance, I will keep you from the hour of trial that is coming on the whole world to test the inhabitants of the earth. I am coming soon; hold fast to what you have, so that no one may seize your crown" (vv. 10-11). There they were, having survived, and no one had "seized their crown."

Then comes that climactic word. "If you conquer, I will make you a pillar in the temple of my God. . . . I will write on you the name of my God, and the name of the city of my God, the new Jerusalem that comes down from my God out of heaven, and my own new name" (v. 12).

The whole world of Christianity outside that Eastern Bloc knows that the suffering church—that church that lived under persecution all those years—is a "pillar in the temple of . . . God." The name of God has been written on that fellowship, and it is a dynamic part of the City of God.

It is easy for me to put my "Revelation experience" together with the word of 1 John: "Who is it that conquers the world but the one who believes that Jesus is the Son of God" (5:5). Let anyone who has an ear listen to what the Spirit is saying to the churches. We can believe it: he set before us "an open door, which no one is able to shut."

QUESTIONS FOR REFLECTION

What doors has God opened in your life in the past? What doors might God be opening for you now? Who do you know who are pillars of faith?

The Grace-Filled Life

50

THE HEART OF THE MATTER

1 JOHN 3:23, 4:1-6; 2 JOHN 4-9

The heart of the matter is a matter of the heart. That's true; but, according to John, the heart of the matter includes the mind. In his Second Letter, he makes that clear to those followers of Christ, and to us also, as followers of Christ. There are no themes in this letter that are not present in his first. John does not have to deal with doctrine, except to call persons to be faithful not to some "phantom Christ" but to Jesus, who came in the flesh, lived among us, was crucified dead, and was buried. This is the Christ in whom we are to believe in order to be saved.

A MATTER OF THE HEART

When we seek the heart of the Christian faith, truth and love are two sides of the same coin. "God's love was revealed among us in this way: God sent his only Son into the world so that we might live through him" (1 John 4:9). This was God's way of speaking for himself in human history—in Christ. "In this is love, not that we loved God, but that he loved us and sent his Son to be the atoning sacrifice for our sins" (1 John 4:10). These parallel sentences are John's expression both of truth and of the nature of love. For John, love is what God has done for us in Jesus Christ. The love to which we are called is to walk with Christ in compassionate care for those around us.

"We love . . . because he first loved us" (1 John 4:19), is an electrifying sentence that is the basis for how we are to live as Christians. Having made the essence of truth and the nature of love clear in his First Letter, John calls for "tough love" in his Second: "And this is love, that we walk according to his commandments" (v. 6). The commandments John is talking about here are those concerning love. This is the heart of the matter.

A mild little boy, not known for being ugly or mean, was being chastised and about to be punished for pulling a little girl's hair. His mother asked him, "Son, why did you do it? That's just not like you."

"Mama," he responded, "I just got tired of being good all the time."

It happens to all of us, doesn't it? That's our problem as we think about the heart of the matter. We get tired of being good and tired of laying our lives on the line for peace and justice, ministry to the poor, reaching out to the least of these. And it's not just getting tired now and then. Being Christian and practicing ministry wears us down. We talk about fatigue in all sorts of ways; what

I'm talking about could be designated "compassion fatigue." Boil it down, re-
fine it to its most precious essence, and you come out with this: to love and
show compassion is the call of every Christian.

The truth is we could open the New Testament at almost any page and find
a similar message as these in John's Letters. Jesus' life, ministry, death, and resurrection were all about love and compassion. This is God's heart: "For God so
loved the world, that he gave his only begotten Son, that whoever believeth
in him should not perish, but have everlasting life" (John 3:16 KJV). That's the
reason we should pray often: "Oh God, break my heart with the things that
break your heart."

This is God's heart. So I could use that summary word of Jesus in the fifteenth chapter of John: "This is my commandment, that you love one another
as I have loved you. No one has greater love than this, to lay down one's life
for one's friends" (vv. 12-13).

Or we could think of that heart-piercing judgment picture of Jesus in
Matthew 24. The basis on which we will be judged is made scathingly
clear:

> Come, you who are blessed by my Father, inherit the Kingdom prepared for you
> from the foundation of the world. For I was hungry and you gave me food, I was
> thirsty and you gave me drink, I was a stranger and you welcomed me, I was
> naked and you clothed me, I was sick and you visited me, I was in prison and you
> came to me. (Matt. 25:34-36 ESV)

So any number of scriptural passages carries this essence of the Christian
gospel and the Christian life—our call to love and compassion. "The love of
God was manifested toward us, that God has sent His only begotten Son into
the world" (1 John 4:9 NKJV). That's incarnation—God becoming one of us,
personally identifying with us. As Earl Palmer has put it: "Love is the person
Jesus Christ, alongside humanity, on the road as Savior of the world" (*The
Communicator's Commentary*, vol. 12, p. 67).

A PRICE TAG

We know what the love of God is only as we look at the cross of Jesus Christ.
But there is more. John concluded, and so must we, in verse 11: "If God so
loved us, we also ought to love one another" (ESV). It can't get any clearer
than that. *Compassion is at the heart of our call to be Christian*—loving *out* of the
love of God, loving *with* the love of God, *continuing* to love until we give up
the last ounce of our being on behalf of the Kingdom.

I don't want to diminish any of this truth and call, but let's recognize a crucial factor in our seeking to live it out. Following Jesus in love carries with it

a price tag, and with it the possibility of fatigue—compassion fatigue. If it has not happened yet, it will. We will grow weary, and there will be occasions when there is no end in sight. There will always be someone standing by to be loved. There will always be a stranger entering our life and causing us to sense that somehow Jesus may be in that stranger. There will be the call in the middle of the night—the request to go the second, even the third mile, to give not only your coat but your cloak as well.

Standing alongside the poor, making our congregations places for recovery folks and the marginalized, championing the cause of single parents and homeless persons—all of this is demanding, requiring not only time and money but also emotional and spiritual energy. We will grow weary. We will suffer compassion fatigue.

WHEN COMPASSION FATIGUE SETS IN

The question is how do we continue in ministry, being Christian, when being Christian has worn us down? How do we live with or prevent total collapse from compassion fatigue?

First, *we must recognize that there is a limit to what we can offer.* This is tough for sincere Christ followers because our love of God sensitizes us to the needs around us. The more we love, the more aware we become of the needs of love. The closer we walk with the Lord, the more our eyes are opened and the more we see the loneliness, the pain, the quiet desperation of people around us. The closer we walk with the Lord, the more tender our hearts become, and we cry within when human needs go unmet.

Yet we must do it. When compassion fatigue begins to set in, simply recognize and acknowledge that there is a limit to what we can offer.

Carry this idea one step further. *Relax in the fact that there is a time to leave to God and to others what we cannot do ourselves.* There are others who share his life and ministry. It is a matter of faith that God will use someone else to minister to those we are not able to love and serve.

Apart from these two principles, an ongoing practice, which will be a great prescription for our dealing with compassion fatigue, is *to regularly renew our strength by waiting on the Lord.* Isaiah put it so beautifully:

> They that wait upon the LORD shall renew their strength; they shall mount up with wings as eagles; they shall run, and not be weary; and they shall walk, and not faint. (40:31 KJV)

We Christians need to realize that we cannot act out of our own strength alone. We must establish a pace in life, a rhythm of engagement and disengagement, being in the world but removing ourselves from the world in order that we might be renewed.

QUESTIONS FOR REFLECTION

Where do you need refreshment and renewal? How difficult is it for you to admit your limitations and weaknesses? Where do you go to get strength to help you persevere?

51

LOCKED IN A ROOM WITH ALL DOORS OPEN

DEUTERONOMY 30:19-20; PSALM 146:1-10

Hans Sachs tells a story about a family of his acquaintance, in which there were two brothers. The younger brother had a terrible dread of open doors. The older brother, wanting to break him of his habit, threatened: "One day I will lock you up in a room with all the doors open." It's a powerful image. Can't you just see that poor boy, who had a dread of open doors—in the middle of a room with every door open—scared to death.

FASCINATION WITH DOORS

Doors are fascinating. If they are closed, we wonder what's behind them. If they are open, we wonder if we would be welcome inside. The door is an intriguing image. Most of us are hesitant about opening strange doors; and for some of us, any barrier, any challenge, any difficulty becomes a closed door. Perhaps less thought about but just as limiting is that there are open doors all around us—doors to fuller life and meaning through which we could go if we would.

Let's use our beginning image, *locked in a room with all doors open*, to reflect on Moses' challenge to Israel and to think about some forces in our life for which we need to find open doors in order to escape. A key verse in the book of Deuteronomy is 30:6: "The LORD your God will circumcise your heart and the heart of your descendants, so that you will love the LORD your God with all your heart and with all your soul, in order that you may live." Circumcision is a biblical metaphor for holiness. It began with God's command to Abraham. But in Deuteronomy, it is clear that God's deepest concern is not physical circumcision but heart circumcision, an obedient love relationship with God.

So Moses called all of Israel together. He had some clear, incisive words he wanted to speak to God's people; and he calls upon all the hosts of heaven and earth to witness the serious situation faced by the people. The issue is clear-cut; compromise is no longer an option; it's time for a decision. So Moses sets before the people of God both life and death, blessing and cursing; and he says to them, "Therefore choose life, that both you and your descendants may live" (Deut. 30:19 NKJV).

When we feel locked in, when we have become immobilized by forces we can't control, we need to choose life—we need to look for the open door.

At any crossroad, whenever "life" and "death" is set before us, our capacity to remember will serve us well in choosing. Moses reminded Israel of this:

> When all these things have happened to you, the blessings and the curses . . . if you call them to mind among all the nations where the LORD your God has driven you, and return to the LORD . . . and . . . obey him with all your heart . . . then the LORD . . . will restore your fortunes and have compassion on you. (Deut. 30:1-3)

It is remembering, and returning to the Lord, that enables us to deal with our fear of the present circumstance as well as what forebodings we have about the future.

SECURE IN CHRIST

Fear immobilizes us when we dwell excessively on it. I've seen it happen with people concerned about their health. They make themselves sick worrying about their health. I've seen it happen with people who are insecure in themselves. They have low self-esteem, and their fear of rejection or disapproval immobilizes them in relationships and prevents them from taking the risks necessary for personal growth.

This locked room of fear is a room with open doors. One of those wide-open doors is trust—the door that calls us to exercise the faith that God cares for each of us, that even the hairs on our head are numbered, that what we need—what we really need—is going to be supplied. Psalm 146 expresses it.

> The LORD sets the prisoners free;
>   the LORD opens the eyes of the blind.
> The LORD lifts up those who are bowed down;
>   the LORD loves the righteous.
> The LORD watches over strangers;
>   he upholds the orphan and the widow,
>   but the way of the wicked he brings to ruin. (vv. 8-10)

When we are locked in the room of fear, we need to remember there is an open door of trust—trust in others, but above all trust in Christ. That door will lead to freedom.

Likewise, many of us are locked in a room of limitation, pain, and suffering. It may be mental, emotional, or physical. Most of us are not strangers to limitations of some sort. We need to realize that it's a room with open doors. My brother-in-law was a great witness to this. He lived with lymphoma for three years before he died. My wife, Jerry, his sister, provided a bone-marrow transplant for him in the midst of his illness, and he lived a year and a half after that transplant. Lymphoma did not conquer Randy—cancer was not the victor—Randy was.

He would write his prayers, many of which he shared with us. Two months before his death he wrote this prayer, which he titled "Prayer of Frustration While in Hospital":

Abba: This [is] so frustrating. You've had me "on hold" for two years now. Just when I think I'm getting better, you jerk the rug from under me by letting me come down with pneumonia. I've been in the hospital now for two weeks and I still have fevers. I pray to you to hurry and get my fever up to 101 so they will give me some Tylenol and my chills will go away.

Father: It's time to stop playing games with me. I have asked you for direction, a sign, a calling as to what you want me to do with the rest of my life, but I hear and see nothing. You said that if I seek I shall find; knock and the door will be opened. I have sought and I have knocked, so far I hear nothing. If you have no plans for me, let me go to you. If you do have plans would you please let me know? And make it soon, Father. I'm not afraid of either. The status quo here, though, is getting tedious and boring. Thank you for indulging me and forgiving my anger.

In all of the three years of suffering, I could not have described Randy in any other way than that he was a person of power. He had discovered power in his brokenness and in his suffering. Power was in his relationship with Christ, a relationship he cultivated through worship, Scripture, prayer, and Christian fellowship. He became aware that the room of limitation, pain, suffering, and fear in which he was locked was really a room with doors, and he could move out of imprisonment to freedom.

Note one other room in which many are locked: the room of destructive lifestyles. If you are locked in such a room, you know it. You are stuck, you think. You can't change. You've been in those ruts too long. We could name some obvious ones: an adulterous relationship, a life of deceit that is filled with fear that you will be found out; a closeted homosexual relationship; destructive gambling, drug, alcohol, or sexual addiction. You know if you are stuck there. You are living as though there is no door out of that room when the door is flung wide open.

It doesn't matter what your destructive lifestyle might be—the delivering, transforming power of Christ is the open door through which you can leave that room in which you think you are locked.

NOT OUT BUT THROUGH

It's a powerful image: locked in a room with open doors. I've said enough about some of the specific rooms to enable you to know where you are. Let me close with a process word and a witness. The *process* word comes from the poet Robert Frost: "The best way out is through." We can't run away from our problems, whatever they are. Trying to crouch back in a room which we feel is locked is not going to work. There is no relief there. We have to face whatever is locking us up. The open door in our locked room is through whatever problems, limitations, fear, suffering, or lifestyle that has us in bondage. Do you get it? The best way *out* is *through*.

In the same week, some time ago, I received two letters from women in prison. Interestingly, one of the women was a member of our church. Her father was a big drug baron in the eastern part of the United States and was convicted and sentenced to life in prison.

As his daughter, my parishioner had a relationship with this man. She knew that he was dealing drugs and that he was going to get caught. I remember when I first met her, she was on the verge of a nervous breakdown because of her anxiety about her father and her relationship with him. She came for counseling. She began to attend our church, and the church was a transforming influence in her life. She professed her faith in Jesus Christ and was baptized. After her father was put in prison, his girlfriend took over his drug kingdom. She was arrested later and, in a plea-bargaining process, implicated my friend. I still believe that my friend is innocent, though she is spending some time in prison.

This has been a growing experience for her. Her letters reflect that. Listen to these two sentences from one of her letters: "I have learned and grown so much. I, too, can see a great witness being molded. Prison hasn't been easy—just worth it." Now that's a woman who is in a locked room, but has found an open door.

The second letter came from a woman I don't know. She's from Memphis and has become a friend of the woman I just talked about. Her letter was a letter of sadness with little glimmer of hope in it.

Dear Dr. Dunnam,
My name is _____. I am in the Federal Prison camp with _____.
She has shared her letters from you with me. They are a real blessing to her and also to me. I am serving a four-month sentence here. I worked at a bank and made some very bad decisions. I am married to a great and very understanding man. I have an eight-year-old daughter who is holding up very well. I am blessed for this, but I am very angry that all this had to happen. I come from a dysfunctional family and never really felt loved. My mother is no longer living but my father is, but he doesn't care if I live or die. It has always been that way. He was either gone or drunk when I was growing up. I come from a family with four sisters and two brothers, and we were all not loved.

She went on to talk about her pain and anger, with no indication that she is finding any open door out of being locked up in herself.

The difference: One has found the truth of Robert Frost: "The best way out is through." Listen to her: "Prison hasn't been easy—just worth it." The other is locked in a room with open doors and has not yet seen those doors, or is unwilling to walk through them. What about you?

QUESTIONS FOR REFLECTION

What are you most afraid of? How is this fear affecting you? Is there a destructive habit from which you need to be delivered? Would a deeper trust in Christ enable you to live with your limitations?

52

SAYING AMEN AND HALLELUJAH

REVELATION 19:1-10; PSALM 150

In his novel *Light in August*, William Faulkner wrote, "That which is destroying the Church is not the outward groping of those within it or the inward groping of those without, but the professionals who control it and have removed the bells from its steeples." I don't know everything Faulkner meant by that, but this seems clear: steeple bells were meant to call people to worship. Worship is at the heart of what the church is about.

RECALLING THE MIGHTY ACTS OF GOD

Worship is remembering. It is summoning up the past into the present. It is rehearsing the mighty acts of God. We live in constant forgetfulness of God, so worship is essential.

When Jesus was spending his last days with his disciples, they celebrated the Passover, that signal event in the Jewish faith when the community recalls God's mighty act of delivering them out of Egyptian bondage. Jesus baptized that Passover with even more poignant meaning, saying to them, "This do in remembrance of me" (Luke 22:19 KJV). He said that to them after he had told them that he was going to the cross. Remembering, we celebrate.

Two words gather up the meaning of celebrating Christ in worship. Those two words are *Amen* and *Hallelujah*. We see it in the Revelation.

John is in exile, a prisoner on the isle of Patmos. In that setting he was given the privilege of hearing the echo of worship of the redeemed of heaven. The very first word that he heard coming from that heavenly worship was *Hallelujah*!

Why hallelujah? The worshipers answer:

Hallelujah!
Salvation and power and glory to our God,
    for his judgments are true and just. . . .
Hallelujah!
For the Lord our God
    the Almighty reigns. (Rev. 19:1-2, 6)

In the midst of that worship of the multitude, John sees the twenty-four elders and the four living creatures fall down and worship God, who is seated on the throne. They shout, "Amen. Hallelujah!"

The Grace-Filled Life

When we remember who God is, and when we rehearse his mighty acts, we can but say, "Amen! Hallelujah!"

TO THE WILL OF GOD

Amen means "so let it be!" When we say amen in our worship, we are saying, "So let it be to the will of God." That's not easy to say. We are self-centered persons. Our sin has distorted the image of God within us. Even when we are sincere about wanting our life to be filled with meaning and count for something, it's not easy to say amen to the will of God.

A lady said to her pastor, "Pastor, I just don't know what to do. I grew up Methodist but became dissatisfied; became a Baptist but that grew old; I've been a Presbyterian and an Episcopalian. I just don't know what I am!" The wise and blunt pastor replied, "Don't worry, my dear, it doesn't matter what label is on an empty bottle!"

Simply being religious is not enough. Genuine worship—saying amen to the will of God—is essential. Worshiping just to have good feelings and to find some comfort or some escape from the world is alien to what true worship is all about.

In worship, we remember that God is; we rehearse God's mighty acts in history; and we say, "Amen, so let it be to the will of God." We seek to discover God's will for our life, and we yield ourselves to God.

THE ALMIGHTY REIGNS

We add to our amen a lilting hallelujah. When we say hallelujah in worship, we are saying, "Salvation and power and glory to our God, / for his judgments are true and just. . . . / Hallelujah! / For the Lord our God / the Almighty reigns."

James S. Stewart inspired my thinking about worship in his commentary on this Revelation passage. He tells of Sir Edward Burne-Jones being present at the funeral service for Robert Browning. But he said afterward that it was too somber for his liking. It did not seem to fit the gallant soul whom they were remembering. "I would have given something," said Burne-Jones, "for a banner or two; and much would I have given if a chorister had come out of the triforium and rent the air with a trumpet" (James S. Stewart, *The Wind of the Spirit* [Nashville: Abingdon, 1969], p. 53). Far too much of Christian worship is devoid of that lyrical note of joy.

African American congregations do this better than the rest of us. Their songs are shouts of joy. At the foundation of those shouts of joy is their memory of the fact that is expressed so poignantly in that spiritual "God Has Brought Us This Far and He's Not Gonna Leave Us Now."

But our hallelujah is not just for what is. What is may not be so good. Some of us come to worship brokenhearted: a loved one has died, a spouse has left us, a child has fallen into the wrong crowd and the future looks pretty grim. We may have lost a job, or we may be struggling with an aged parent and no decision we make is going to make everybody happy. We are weeping over the loss of lives in war, and despair of any possibility of peace. The news won't let us forget the suffering of the poor and marginalized. So we don't come in joy—we don't come ready to praise God for what is. But we can come to praise God for what can be.

The psalmist asked the question, "How could we sing the LORD's song / in a foreign land?" (137:4). That question is often on our hearts because where we live and what goes on in our life often seems bereft of God's presence. But in worship we bring the past into the present. We celebrate the fact that what has been in the past can be again. In fact, we come in confidence, knowing that God has acted to deliver in the past, so God will deliver us now. He has not brought us this far to forsake us.

So these are the words that give content to our worship. Amen! Hallelujah. Amen: So let it be to the will of God. Hallelujah: Praise to the Lord God, Almighty.

And remember this. Our worship is not a one-time, one-place, one-way kind of thing. Psalm 150 is our guide. Where is God to be praised? "Praise God in his sanctuary; / praise him in his mighty firmament" (v. 1). Why is God to be praised? "Praise him for his mighty deeds; / praise him according to his surpassing greatness!" (v. 2). How is God to be praised? "Praise him with trumpet sound / . . . with lute and harp / . . . with tambourine and dance / . . . with strings and pipe / . . . with loud clashing cymbals" (vv. 3-5). By whom is God to be praised? "Let everything that breathes praise the LORD!" (v. 6).

QUESTIONS FOR REFLECTION

Does your participation in corporate worship enable you to say amen and hallelujah? Apart from corporate worship, where can you say hallelujah and amen in your life? Reflecting over this book of devotions, how has God spoken to you?

The Grace-Filled Life

Appendix
Bible One-Year Reading Plan

Week	The Law Mon.	History Tues.	Psalms Wed.	Poetry Thurs.	Prophets Fri.	Gospels Sat.	Epistles Sun.
1	Gen 1–3	Josh 1–5	Pss 1–2	Job 1–2	Isa 1–6	Matt 1–2	Rom 1–2
2	Gen 4–7	Josh 6–10	Pss 3–5	Job 3–4	Isa 7–11	Matt 3–4	Rom 3–4
3	Gen 8–11	Josh 11–15	Pss 6–8	Job 5–6	Isa 12–17	Matt 5–7	Rom 5–6
4	Gen 12–15	Josh 16–20	Pss 9–11	Job 7–8	Isa 18–22	Matt 8–10	Rom 7–8
5	Gen 16–19	Josh 21–24	Pss 12–14	Job 9–10	Isa 23–28	Matt 11–13	Rom 9–10
6	Gen 20–23	Judg 1–6	Pss 15–17	Job 11–12	Isa 29–33	Matt 14–16	Rom 11–12
7	Gen 24–27	Judg 7–11	Pss 18–20	Job 13–14	Isa 34–39	Matt 17–19	Rom 13–14
8	Gen 28–31	Judg 12–16	Pss 21–23	Job 15–16	Isa 40–44	Matt 20–22	Rom 15–16
9	Gen 32–35	Judg 17–21	Pss 24–26	Job 17–18	Isa 45–50	Matt 23–25	1 Cor 1–2
10	Gen 36–39	Ruth	Pss 27–29	Job 19–20	Isa 51–55	Matt 26–28	1 Cor 3–4
11	Gen 40–43	1 Sam 1–6	Pss 30–32	Job 21–22	Isa 56–61	Mark 1–2	1 Cor 5–6
12	Gen 44–47	1 Sam 7–10	Pss 33–35	Job 23–24	Isa 62–66	Mark 3–4	1 Cor 7–8
13	Gen 48–50	1 Sam 11–15	Pss 36–38	Job 25–26	Jer 1–5	Mark 5–6	1 Cor 9–10
14	Exod 1–4	1 Sam 16–20	Pss 39–41	Job 27–28	Jer 6–11	Mark 7–8	1 Cor 11–12
15	Exod 5–8	1 Sam 21–25	Pss 42–44	Job 29–30	Jer 12–16	Mark 9–10	1 Cor 13–14
16	Exod 9–12	1 Sam 26–31	Pss 45–47	Job 31–32	Jer 17–21	Mark 11–12	1 Cor 15–16
17	Exod 13–16	2 Sam 1–4	Pss 48–50	Job 33–34	Jer 22–26	Mark 13–14	2 Cor 1–3
18	Exod 17–20	2 Sam 5–9	Pss 51–53	Job 35–36	Jer 27–31	Mark 15–16	2 Cor 4–5
19	Exod 21–24	2 Sam 10–14	Pss 54–56	Job 37–38	Jer 32–36	Luke 1–2	2 Cor 6–8
20	Exod 25–28	2 Sam 15–19	Pss 57–59	Job 39–40	Jer 37–41	Luke 3–4	2 Cor 9–10

Week	The Law Mon.	History Tues.	Psalms Wed.	Poetry Thurs.	Prophets Fri.	Gospels Sat.	Epistles Sun.
21	Exod 29–32	2 Sam 20–24	Pss 60–62	Job 41–42	Jer 42–46	Luke 5–6	2 Cor 11–13
22	Exod 33–36	1 Kgs 1–4	Pss 63–65	Prov 1	Jer 47–52	Luke 7–8	Gal 1–3
23	Exod 37–40	1 Kgs 5–9	Pss 66–68	Prov 2–3	Lam	Luke 9–10	Gal 4–6
24	Lev 1–3	1 Kgs 10–13	Pss 69–71	Prov 4	Ezek 1–6	Luke 11–12	Eph 1–3
25	Lev 4–5	1 Kgs 14–18	Pss 72–74	Prov 5–6	Ezek 7–12	Luke 13–14	Eph 4–6
26	Lev 7–9	1 Kgs 19–22	Pss 75–77	Prov 7–8	Ezek 13–18	Luke 15–16	Phil 1–3
27	Lev 10–12	2 Kgs 1–5	Pss 78–80	Prov 9	Ezek 19–24	Luke 17–18	Phil 4
28	Lev 13–15	2 Kgs 6–10	Pss 81–83	Prov 10–11	Ezek 25–30	Luke 19–20	Col 1–2
29	Lev 16–18	2 Kgs 11–15	Pss 84–86	Prov 12	Ezek 31–36	Luke 21–22	Col 3–4
30	Lev 19–21	2 Kgs 16–20	Pss 87–89	Prov 13–14	Ezek 37–42	Luke 23–24	1 Thess 1–3
31	Lev 22–24	2 Kgs 21–25	Pss 90–92	Prov 15	Ezek 43–48	John 1–2	1 Thess 4–5
32	Lev 25–27	1 Chr 1–4	Pss 93–95	Prov 16	Dan 1–6	John 3–4	2 Thess
33	Num 1–4	1 Chr 5–9	Pss 96–98	Prov 17–18	Dan 7–12	John 5–6	1 Tim 1–3
34	Num 5–8	1 Chr 10–14	Pss 99–102	Prov 19	Hos 1–7	John 7–9	1 Tim 4–6
35	Num 9–12	1 Chr 15–19	Pss 103–104	Prov 20–21	Hos 8–14	John 10–12	2 Tim 1–2
36	Num 13–16	1 Chr 20–24	Pss 105–107	Prov 22	Joel	John 13–15	2 Tim 3–4
37	Num 17–20	1 Chr 25–29	Pss 108–110	Prov 23–24	Amos 1–4	John 16–18	Titus
38	Num 21–24	2 Chr 1–5	Pss 111–113	Prov 25	Amos 5–9	John 19–21	Philm
39	Num 25–28	2 Chr 6–10	Pss 114–116	Prov 26–27	Obad	Acts 1–2	Heb 1–4
40	Num 29–32	2 Chr 11–15	Pss 117–118	Prov 28	Jonah	Acts 3–4	Heb 5–7
41	Num 33–36	2 Chr 16–20	Pss 119	Prov 29–30	Mic	Acts 5–6	Heb 8–10
42	Deut 1–3	2 Chr 21–24	Pss 120–121	Prov 31	Nah	Acts 7–8	Heb 11–13

Week	The Law Mon.	History Tues.	Psalms Wed.	Poetry Thurs.	Prophets Fri.	Gospels Sat.	Epistles Sun.
43	Deut 4–6	2 Chr 25–28	Pss 122–124	Eccl 1–2	Hab	Acts 9–10	Jam 1–3
44	Deut 7–9	2 Chr 29–32	Pss 125–127	Eccl 3–4	Zeph	Acts 11–12	Jam 4–5
45	Deut 10–12	2 Chr 33–36	Pss 128–130	Eccl 5–6	Hag	Acts 13–14	1 Pet 1–3
46	Deut 13–15	Ezra 1–5	Pss 131–133	Eccl 7–8	Zech 1–7	Acts 15–16	1 Pet 4–5
47	Deut 16–19	Ezra 6–10	Pss 134–136	Eccl 9–10	Zech 8–14	Acts 17–18	2 Pet
48	Deut 20–22	Neh 1–4	Pss 137–139	Eccl 11–12	Mal	Acts 19–20	1 John 1–3
49	Deut 23–25	Neh 5–9	Pss 140–142	Song 1–2	Rev 1–6	Acts 21–22	1 John 4–5
50	Deut 26–28	Neh 10–13	Pss 143–145	Song 3–4	Rev 7–11	Acts 23–24	2 John
51	Deut 29–31	Esth 1–5	Pss 146–148	Song 5–6	Rev 12–17	Acts 25–26	3 John
52	Deut 32–34	Esth 6–10	Pss 149–150	Song 7–8	Rev 18–22	Acts 27–28	Jude